MW00333919

VIBE

cafe + juicery

Over 50 plant-based recipes from the kitchens of VIBE cafe

—

—

GOOD VIBES. ALL DAY. EVERY DAY.

—

VIBE COOKBOOK

Tested by over half a million customers.

All original recipes developed by our professional vegan chefs.

Twenty five percent of the proceeds of this cookbook will go towards The Good Vibe Foundation, who aim to provide healthy food for school children in Cambodia.

CONTENTS

INTRODUCTION
—

INGREDIENTS & TECHNIQUES
—

RECIPES
—

FOUNDATION
—

A NOTE FROM
OUR FOUNDER

—

When beginning the process of writing this cookbook, it became apparent to me that VIBE is a labor of love and passion for many people from our creators to our customers and it is an absolute honor to be involved in writing it.

We have tried to curate some of our best selling dishes at VIBE and translate them into a format that is easy for you to recreate at home. We made sure to include recipes that could be used in your everyday cooking as the building blocks to a healthier way of eating. For example, our dressings can be used with various salads, our fermented pickles can be added as a condiment with any dish you're preparing and of course our nut butter can be spread on everything in sight! We know that it might seem daunting to be preparing all your food from scratch but the goal is to integrate changes slowly and any steps you take towards eating healthier are steps in the right direction, no matter what your budget or skill level.

My personal food philosophy was formed in my childhood; my family are horticulturalists so we always had freshly picked seasonal vegetables at our table and there would always be a home cooked meal from scratch every evening shared as a family. I started working in restaurants when I was fourteen years old and I even made the food for over fifty guests at my eighteenth birthday party ~ not very rock and roll for a young person! After I studied a sports and nutrition university degree, my love affair with healthy food continued and the restaurant industry just seemed like a natural fit for me.

I'm incredibly lucky to have worked alongside my brother for over ten years now and the journey to developing the concept of VIBE has been shaped from the other cafe concepts we have created, learning what works (and what doesn't) and what people want when they walk in the door of your cafe.

We were motivated to start VIBE in Cambodia as we had a personal connection to the country and its beautiful people and wanted to tie together our love of nutritious plant-based food, the desire to create a beautiful space for people and to give back to the local community.

I'm particularly interested in the domino effect of a guest leaving the cafe feeling energised and happy, smiling at a stranger on the street, going home and cooking healthy food for their family and generally spreading the good vibes. I'm inspired by my endless travels to different cultures, the people I meet, other restaurants I eat at and landscapes and nature will often influence dishes on the menu. Carolina and I have traveled to many countries and absorbed inspiration from all around us.

We always had a plan to grow the business internationally to offer healthy food to more people in the world and we are overwhelmed our dream is happening with the help of our wonderful customers. The feedback we get from guests is the reason we keep on doing what we do. Our goal has always been to make people happy through food.

My advice to anyone contemplating opening their own cafe would be ~ be prepared to work really hard, focus on every small detail and respect your team.

Sending you good vibes, all day, everyday.

Emma | Founder

OUR PHILOSOPHY

Vibe / vīb / noun / informal
A person's emotional state or the atmosphere of a place as communicated to and felt by others.

VIBE SPIRIT

Our name VIBE was inspired by the amazing vibration of bee's wings when they visit flowers to collect pollen; the high vibrational effect of the earth as it grows our food by the seasons and the vibe we experience when we have a connection with other people.

YOU ARE WHAT YOU EAT

Food doesn't just fuel our body, it impacts how we feel throughout the day. What we eat affects our digestive health, skin radiance, energy levels but also our emotional body, our mood and motivation. We wanted a cafe concept which embraced, wholeheartedly, the powerful connection between mind and body. Our plant-based recipes are specifically designed using the healthiest of ingredients to extract the maximum nutritional value. We wanted to avoid faux health foods like tofu and focus instead on whole foods from the earth that we know are nutrient-rich and know exactly where they come from. We believe eating a plant-based diet is the optimal way to nourish and care for the body and mind.

POSITIVE VIBES

The VIBE experience is nearly as much an aesthetic and a lifestyle as it is a cuisine. Everything is mindfully curated to promote a sense of harmony and balance. We want people to leave the cafe feeling more positive, more energized and inspired by the world around them.

A TASTE FOR HEALTH

Bland, tasteless, too wholesome, unappetizing to the eye are just some of the common misconceptions around healthy plant-based food. At VIBE we work with the very best plant-based chefs to create vibrant, truly nourishing dishes bursting with energy and flavor. Every dish is made from ethically sourced ingredients, consciously and carefully chosen. We care so much about what goes into every dish that we make almost everything in-house using techniques to maximum the nutritional quality of the food.

GOOD FOOD. GOOD VIBES.

At VIBE we like to keep it simple which is why we focus on those things that matter most to us - good food and good vibes. We believe food should be an experience, always vibrant, truly nourishing, made from plant-based ingredients which have been consciously and ethically sourced. More than a cafe, we create a space where people can recharge and restore both inside and out. We give people a chance to experience what a healthy lifestyle looks, feels and tastes like.

LIVING CONSCIOUSLY

We care about our impact on the environment. Which is why we aim to be plastic free by 2020 and why we only use eco-friendly cleaning products, biodegradable packaging and all our wooden furniture is made from reclaimed and recycled materials.

OUR FOOD PHILOSOPHY

Honest food, just as mother nature intended – no shortcuts, no chemicals, no compromise.

PLANT-BASED

Natural, chemical free food that feeds our heart as well as our body is central to VIBE's DNA. We believe that respecting the ingredients makes the food taste better, cleaner and more vibrant somehow, like its showing us love.

We simply believe that 'eating the rainbow' of food grown in nature provides us with an abundance of essential nutrients, minerals and fiber we need to feel alive and vibrant. The phytonutrient compound found in the chemicals of plants contain bioactive components that have been proven to reduce cellular inflammation, fight disease and promote immunity.

Our bodies need a wide variety of fruit and vegetables for us to operate at optimum well-being. We believe that the more intense the natural color of fruit, vegetables and everything else that comes from the earth, the greater energetic properties they contain which in turn positively impacts our physical and energetic bodies.

Plant-based for us is not only embodying the 'earth to table' approach but also extracting nutrients from food to improve brain chemistry, help fight disease, enhance mood, elevate skin appearance and boost energy levels.

FROM SCRATCH

We live in a world of ultra-convenience, mostly because we are overworked and time poor. When it comes to creating nourishing, plant-based food from 'earth to table' we like to take our time to get it right.

We are dedicated and committed to producing 99% of our food in-house. This means we make nearly everything from scratch in our kitchens, including our sauces, dressings, pickles, milks and cheeses. No artificial preservatives are used in the making of our food. You will see in the recipes of this cookbook that we even make our own nut butters, jams, syrups and infusions using whole foods.

Our plant-based chefs work hard to ensure we extract the maximum nutritional value from all our recipes ~ from soaking, activating and fermenting, we do our best to get the most from every single ingredient.

ETHICAL AND ORGANIC

We pride ourselves on creating nutritious, plant-based dishes in the most natural way possible, focusing on honest ingredients that are locally and ethically sourced. Although in Cambodia it's difficult to source all organic ingredients, we work closely with local farmers and suppliers to ensure we are getting the highest quality ingredients available. We advocate for you to buy the best quality products you can afford and to do your research on what ingredients are in season in your area.

It's really exciting for us to find a local artisan or grower who is dedicated and has an original product we can use in our dishes and it also creates community and supports independent businesses.

INGREDIENTS
& TECHNIQUES

GLUTEN FREE

Although not all our dishes are gluten free at VIBE, we do try to offer mostly dishes that are naturally gluten free and we are always looking for whole food alternatives to using traditional refined flours and grains.

WHAT IS GLUTEN?
—

Gluten is the general name for the proteins found in some grains such as wheat, rye, spelt and barley. It is made up of two different classes of proteins: gliadin, which gives bread the ability to rise during baking, and glutenin, which is responsible for dough's elasticity.

WHY GLUTEN FREE?
—

Nowadays it is very common for those even without gluten sensitivities to avoid gluten. Some people feel lighter and clearer without gluten and it is a personal preference. Those with celiac disease or other forms of gluten intolerance need to cut gluten entirely from their diet.

FOODS CONTAINING GLUTEN
—

Gluten is hidden in many common pre-made foods you can buy from the supermarket. It is important to read labels, inform yourself of gluten in its many forms: it is commonly in breads, baked goods, soups, pasta, sauces, salad dressings, food coloring, beer, soups, and cereals, etc.

GLUTEN FREE ALTERNATIVES
—

Cutting out gluten from your diet may seem difficult but there are many delicious options that are naturally gluten free such as fruit, vegetables, beans, legumes, nuts, seeds, cassava and corn. Swap flour to almond, buckwheat or coconut flour and you can try amaranth, chickpea, millet, quinoa, teff, tapioca, etc.

Just because a product is gluten free doesn't mean it's healthy. It can still be highly processed and refined, so for this reason at VIBE, we put focus on whole foods, proper healthy fats, proteins and fiber.

SWEETENERS

When it comes to sweeteners, we believe the less refined the better. We use the natural sweetness of fruits, dates and coconuts in a lot of our dishes. Below are the other sweeteners we use regularly. You can also use many other vegan alternatives such as agave, yacon syrup, molasses and brown rice syrup.

MAPLE SYRUP
—

Is made by boiling down the sap of maple trees. When purchasing syrup, be sure it is labeled "maple syrup", rather than "maple flavored" or "pancake syrup", as these are usually not 100% maple and are mixed with corn syrup and other products with poor nutritional value.

It has a distinct flavor that pairs very well with chocolate. Pure maple syrup is filled with potassium, magnesium, zinc and iron, among other minerals.

It dehydrates well to create crisp recipes, such as candied nuts and granolas.

DATES
—

If we are judging dates by their nutritional profile, it might be easy to categorize them as candy rather than fruit, but with plenty of potassium, magnesium, and fiber and its delicious caramel flavor, dates are one of our favorite unrefined, whole food natural sweeteners.

Medjool is our favorite variety, for its texture; not too chewy / not too soft and its rich flavor and intense sweetness.

If you are using dried dates, you may need to soak them in warm water until they are tender for better incorporation into recipes and to aid in digestion.

PALM AND COCONUT SUGAR
—

Palm sugar and coconut sugar are both natural sweeteners that come from trees: coconut sugar, from the buds of coconut tree flowers and palm sugar made from the sap of sugar palm tree.

They have a distinctive flavor similar to brown sugar, fruit, sweet, tart, a nice caramel-like taste which is similar to natural molasses but lighter.

The unrefined organic versions are best, containing micronutrients and minerals like iron, zinc, calcium, and potassium, as well as inulin fiber.

LUCUMA
—

Made from lucuma, a tropical fruit native to Peru, Chili and Ecuador. It has exceptional nutritional value and anti-aging properties but is also known for its subtle sweet flavor that adds creaminess and richness to raw desserts and smoothies.

MESQUITE
—

A traditional spiny tree that grows in New Mexico, Arizona and California. Mesquite bean flour has a rich caramel taste and nutty flavor, often used in raw desserts and smoothies. It goes really well with cinnamon, cacao, carob, maca, vanilla and other sweet spices.

// TIPS

We share this recipe as an example of how you can build your own sweeteners.

HOMEMADE COCONUT SYRUP
—

INGREDIENTS

1000g coconut water

500g palm sugar

METHOD

In a medium saucepan, bring to a boil coconut water and sugar, stirring until the sugar dissolves. Reduce to medium heat and simmer for about 40 minutes. Remove from the heat and leave the syrup to cool.

Store in a container in the refrigerator for up to 2 weeks.

NUTS & SEEDS

We use a great deal of nuts and seeds in our kitchens, they are essential for plant-based cuisine as they're the basis of our milks, raw desserts and cheeses. We always buy them raw and roast ourselves when needed to ensure that the natural oils don't go rancid.

CASHEWS

Have a high content of monounsaturated fats and minerals including copper, magnesium, thiamine, calcium, and niacin.

In VIBE's kitchen we use cashews for their rich texture, and their sweet and buttery notes in many savory recipes such as "cheesy mayo" (see recipe, page 49), "sour cream" (see recipe, page 57), to prepare cheese, desserts such as "tiramisu" (see recipe, page 90) and it is our favorite milk.

ALMONDS

Almond seeds (often called nuts) are a very rich source of concentrated nutrients, rich in vitamin E, calcium, phosphorus, magnesium and iron.

We use almonds raw, blanched and roasted, converted into flour, butter and milk in a variety of recipes such as "almond feta cheese" (see recipe, page 66), in our "granola" (see recipe, page 34) and activated as toppings in our bowls.

FLAXSEEDS

Also known as linseed, they come in brown and gold varieties with an earthy and mildly nutty flavor. They are one of the richest sources of essential fatty acids and a good source of dietary fiber. It's better if you consume them as oil and ground into meal, rather than eating them whole. Flaxseed meal and oil are particularly prone to oxidation so must be stored in the refrigerator to keep fresh.

We use flax and chia seeds to replace eggs in recipes such as "eggless green omelette" (see recipe, page 44) and "peanut butter cookie" (see recipe, page 83). As a guide, use 1 tablespoon of ground flaxseed soaked in 3 tablespoons of warm water for 10-15 minutes.

SESAME SEEDS

Are one of the most ancient foods on earth, highly used in Asian, Mediterranean and African cultures, adding a distinctive and delicate nutty flavor in a variety of recipes either as they are, or made into oil or paste.

SUNFLOWER SEEDS

Come from the beautiful sunflower plant, and like sesame and pumpkin, have a powerful health punch. They are rich in nutrients, healthy fats, vitamin E, B, zinc, phosphorus, iron and low in carbohydrates.

PUMPKIN SEEDS

Like nuts, pumpkin seeds (usually called by their Mexican name of pepitas) are a great source of protein and unsaturated fats, including omega-3. They are also an excellent source of magnesium and zinc. You can roast them, candy them, spice them, make pesto, add them to granola, make dressings, garnish salads and prepare nut free bars.

// TIPS

The natural oils in nuts and seeds go rancid within a few months, so buy nuts raw, unsalted, and whole in small quantities and store in sealed containers in a cool, dark place. Once opened, it is a good idea to store nuts and seeds in the freezer or fridge. They will last longer in a colder place. Nuts take on other flavors easily, so store away from high odor foods.

OILS, VINEGARS & OTHER LIQUIDS

In VIBE kitchens, we use different cooking oils to suit flavor and cooking temperature requirements. Choosing the right oil can be overwhelming when there is a whole aisle at your local grocery store offering a multitude of options. We recommend having two or three oils on hand for different uses.

OLIVE, EXTRA VIRGIN
—

Extra virgin means unrefined, free of chemicals and never treated with heat. We use good quality extra virgin oil for roasting, making vinaigrettes, dressing vegetables and finishing. Olive oils are not neutral in flavor, they can range from spicy to fruity depending on their origins. When buying olive oil, don't buy blended oils, and stay away from terms like light or pure.

COCONUT, COLD PRESSED, VIRGIN
—

We use it as a setting agent, and for flavor and aroma in savory and sweet dishes. We only use coconut oil with minimal processing, which has been extracted using a wet method centrifuge extraction process. This ensures its smoothness, lightness and maximum nutritional nourishment.

OIL FOR HIGH HEAT
—

A neutral, refined oil with a high smoke point, such as sunflower or grapeseed oil, is also essential. These oils are used for deep frying because olive oil is not ideal for high heat cooking. An oils 'smoke point' is precisely what it sounds like - the temperature at which the oil shifts from shimmering to smoking. When oil begins to smoke, free radicals release, giving the oil and the food you are cooking a burnt, bitter flavor as well as degrading its nutritional value.

FINISHING OIL
—

One other oil you may enjoy keeping in your toolkit is a finishing oil. Finishing oils are rich and delicate, so they should not be used with heat, just only as a drizzle to finish a dish or enhance a vinaigrette. At VIBE, we use toasted sesame oil in our Asian inspired dishes and to enhance our tahini recipe. It is highly perishable, so store it in the refrigerator.

APPLE CIDER VINEGAR
—

Vinegar made from crushed apples fermented in wooden barrels is used at VIBE in many recipes from drinks to sauces, pickles and desserts.

Apple cider vinegar is one of the best kitchen remedies. Choose organic, raw cider vinegar, preferably with the mother culture. It offers a great deal of cleansing benefits, including promoting weight loss, boosting energy, lowering blood sugar, and relieving indigestion. It can also be used topically as a hair wash and potent skin cleanser. Apple cider vinegar is truly a pantry staple.

RICE VINEGAR
—

Made from fermented rice, it is less acidic and tends to have a mild and sweet taste compared with some other vinegars. We use it in combination with apple cider vinegar in pickles and dressings to add a subtle flavor and a stimulating contrast.

BALSAMIC VINEGAR
—

Made from grapes that ferment in oak barrels. The flavor is sweet, sour, rich and syrupy. It lends a richness in our dressings and sauces.

TAMARI
—

Traditionally tied to Japanese cooking, versus the more common Chinese soy sauce. It is thicker, less salty, fermented soy sauce made with no, or very little, wheat. Tamari tends to be sweeter and has a more complex flavor than soy sauce. At VIBE we use it to add full, savory, umami flavor to our dishes.

// TIPS

Oils are the most sensitive wet pantry item in your kitchen. They should be stored in a cool, dark place or in the refrigerator in a dark colored glass, ceramic or non-reactive metal container. Avoid storing in plastic containers because chemicals from the plastic can seep into the oil. Keep away from your stove, windows or any warm place.

SUPERFOODS

We believe that all natural foods are super but some foods have a denser concentration of nutrients and antioxidants than others and are classed as 'superfoods'. As the health food scene develops, there are new superfoods popping up all the time.

The term superfood has been around quite a while, but it has gained popularity over the last decade. Superfoods comprise a class of food that give us a considerable concentration of micronutrients and other elements such as vitamins, minerals, antioxidants, amino acids, essential fatty acids, phytonutrients, and fiber, and at the same time only give us a small calorie content. Adding even one superfood to your diet can bolster your health in many positive ways, no matter what your diet, age, or status of health.

CHIA SEEDS

—

Are tiny black seeds from the plant Salvia Hispanica, which is related to mint and grows natively in South America. These tiny seeds are packed with a powerful nutritional punch, containing essential fatty acids, dietary fiber and are high in antioxidants, a powerhouse of vitamins, minerals, including calcium, phosphorus, manganese and protein. Chia seeds can be used much like flaxseed as an egg replacement, because of their mucilaginous quality when soaked with any liquid, also they are especially good to use as a thickening agent in recipes like puddings, soups and smoothies; or sprinkled in salad and incorporated into bread doughs.

MACA

—

The maca plant has grown in the high altitudes of the Andes of Peru and for thousands of years, maca roots have been used by native Indians in Peru for medicinal and health benefits. It is legendary for delivering energy, mental clarity and enhancing libido. Maca is rich in vitamins B, C, and E and provides a good dose of amino acids, calcium, zinc, magnesium, iron, and phosphorous. It is also used as an aphrodisiac to increase libido and endurance. Maca balances the body's delicate endocrine system, acting on the pituitary gland to regulate and balance all the hormonal systems in the body, including thyroid and adrenals, supporting natural energy and vitality. It can be mixed easily into smoothies, juices, baked goods, pancakes, ice creams, and chocolate.

GOJI BERRIES

—

Wolfberries, commercially called goji berries, have a long history of use in traditional Chinese medicine for over 2000 years, are high in vitamin C and fiber and are known as a secret to longevity, balancing hormones, strengthen the immune system, lowering blood pressure, easing inflammation, and promoting healthy skin, among a list of other benefits.

Wondering how goji berries taste compared to other berries and fruits? Their taste is a special sweet / tart and slightly salty 'bite', a combination between a cherry, cranberry, raisin, and tomato, with a chewy texture and a bright pink color. We love using them in our granola, smoothies and tonics.

ACAI

—

Comes from the acai palm tree, native to Central and South America and it is a great source of antioxidants like resveratrol, minerals and vitamins including B, K, potassium, manganese, calcium, copper, magnesium, and zinc. In addition, acai lowers cholesterol and increases heart health, supports healthy skin, aids digestion, boosts the immune system, improves mental focus, and promotes anti-aging.

SPIRULINA

—

Is cyanobacteria (blue-green algae) that is considered to be one of the most potent foods on the planet! Spirulina is known as a nutrient-dense food as it is packed full of vitamins, including vitamins A, B1, B2, B3, B6, B9, C, D and E, is high in antioxidants and chlorophyll, rich in protein, and as well as a whole host of minerals such as calcium, potassium, chromium, copper, magnesium, manganese, phosphorus, sodium, selenium, and zinc. It is also a highly absorbable source of iron.

As it has a strong and oceany taste, a little goes a long way. You can sneak it into smoothies, energy bars, ice cream, and puréed soups. At VIBE, we add it in our superfood green pesto as when it's combined with other strong flavors such as basil and peanuts you can't taste it.

CACAO

—

Cacao, or "Theobroma cacao", is native to South America, and grown in equatorial regions worldwide. It comes from seeds of the fruit of the cacao tree and it is the source of all original, natural chocolate. Organic raw cacao is a superfood containing a variety of unique phytonutrients that provide many benefits, it helps neutralize free radicals, balances brain chemistry, promotes focus and alertness, and is a great mood enhancer.

ADAPTOGENS

Adaptogens have been used in traditional medicine for over a thousand years but they are now just becoming popular again in the modern day fight against anxiety, fatigue and insomnia. We often turn to caffeine and sugar to combat these issues, but they can do more damage than good. Fortunately, there are healthier ways to get through the day.

An adaptogen is a unique group of herbal ingredients which are used for medicinal purposes. For a herb to qualify as an adaptogen it must be completely safe, non toxic and have a variety of uses that can improve the health of people taking it. In addition to this they must help specifically reduce stress, both, mentally and physically.

SO HOW DID WE COME TO DESCRIBE THESE HERBS AS ADAPTOGENS?

Adaptogens weren't born yesterday. The concept of plants with restorative properties that can enhance health has been around for thousands of years in Ayurveda and traditional Chinese medicine, although the concept of adaptogens was first introduced in the late 1940s with the need to increase stamina, endurance, and performance of soldiers, pilots, sailors, and civilians engaged in production of weapons and war material.

HOW DO ADAPTOGENS WORK?

Thanks to their unusual influence on our ability to handle stress, adaptogens can offer a unique way to support your health. An adaptogen works in a bidirectional manner, meaning they work in two directions, for example, there are adaptogenic substances that come from certain special herbs, that if you have high blood pressure when you take it, the pressure drops and if you have low blood pressure, when you take it the pressure rises. It means that it helps balance the body and adapt the bodies condition.

They can offer you a way to support your best possible health and performance, but moderation is key. Do not forget that adaptogens promote health, but they should not be a substitute for good self care practices.

It is true that adaptogens and other herbs are all natural, but it's always a good idea to consult with your primary health care provider before including adaptogens in your diet. Your current state of health and your health history are important considerations when deciding to incorporate any herbs into your diet, and it's especially true of adaptogens.

WATCH SERVING SIZES

When you add herbs to your diet, it's important to remember that more isn't necessarily better. They are safe herbs, but any supplementation requires some caution. Taking too much of one or more at the same time or over the course of a day can leave you feeling nervy. With prepackaged herbs it's important to follow the recommended serving size and directions that come with the product.

ASHWAGANDHA

Is an adaptogen that has a reputation as a nerve soother. Nervous system health challenges such as anxiety, fatigue and insomnia from stress are all good reasons to consider ashwagandha. It is a super herb with many other properties: it appears to enhance endocrine function; it can be supportive during heavy periods because it is rich in iron and it is an immune, fertility and antispasmodic tonic.

CORDYCEPS

Is a type of fungus regularly prescribed to support the bodies immune system. Traditionally used to support the health of the kidneys, cordyceps is used as an all illnesses tonic because it improves energy, appetite, stamina, libido, and fatigue. More modern applications include the use for athletic performance.

BURDOCK

Is another hormone balancing superfood that helps to detoxify the blood, aids in digestion, removes excess hormones and cleanses the liver and also is used for skin conditions such as acne, eczema and psoriasis.

GOTU KOLA

Also known as Centella asiatica, a wonderful herb to use if you are looking for an adaptogen that supports mental clarity and focus. The leaves have been used to boost cognition, increase memory, longevity, improve cerebral circulation, and overall brain function. It is also a powerful blood purifier and is commonly used in Ayurveda to treat chronic skin diseases.

SCHISANDRA BERRIES

Considered a calming adaptogen with an effect on the nervous systems. Besides being calming and helping to relieve anxiety, it also enhances reflexes and improves concentration and coordination.

TECHNIQUES

When working with living food, it's important for us to keep the integrity of the ingredients and work with them gently to preserve and extract the maximum nutritional benefits of the produce. The techniques we apply to our food have an impact on how we are able to digest the food and how bioavailable the nutrition is to us. This is a very brief overview but there are many wonderful detailed books available on these topics if you want to dive deeper.

ACTIVATING

Soaking nuts and seeds in filtered water and dehydrating them at low temperatures unlocks the nutritional potential inside them. They naturally contain phytic acid which inhibits the ability to absorb certain minerals. It can bind to minerals such as zinc, iron and magnesium making them unavailable to our bodies. They also contain enzyme inhibitors which can block their function. Activating nuts and seeds also makes them easier for us to digest. Different nuts and seeds require different soaking times. You can find this information easily on the internet for whichever nut you are using. You can even soak nuts and seeds for as little as 10 minutes before eating them as a snack. Be sure to discard the water you soaked them in and rinse them with clean water before eating.

DEHYDRATING

Is the process of extracting moisture from food to preserve it for longer. The advantage of dehydrating food below 40°C (104°F) is that it keeps the nutritional value of the food. We know that not everyone will have a dehydrator at home, and although we believe it is a worthy investment, you can do a similar function in your oven if you set it to very low temperatures for long periods of time. The advantage of a dehydrator is that it's precise and automated and you can dry several things at once.

FERMENTING

We love to ferment at VIBE. It is the process of lacto-fermentation which preserves the nutritional content of food. It produces bacteria that is more readily available to the body and the bacteria also produces enzymes that are beneficial for digestion and are known for improving gut health. Be sure to keep all your equipment sterilized and clean to prevent spoilage.

SPROUTING

You can sprout nuts, seeds, legumes, and grains. It is achieved by soaking them for several hours, then rinsing repeatedly until they start to grow a 'tail'. The benefit of sprouting is that it enhances the bioavailability of their nutrients and can be more gentle on digestion. We love to include sprouts on our dishes as they contain a high content of living enzymes.

TOOLS & EQUIPMENT

There are many tools that go into a professional kitchen but here are some of our favorites we think you could use at home - high speed blender, food processor, good quality vegetable knife, mandoline, measuring cups, measuring spoons and nut milk bag.

TRICKS OF THE TRADE

Start early, mise en place your ingredients (meaning prepare all the ingredients and dishes you will need for a particular recipe before you commence making it), batch your cooking, check what needs soaking for the next day, keep your workspace clean and organized, and label and date your food.

// NUT & SEED MILKS

Nut and seed milks are a versatile and invaluable ingredient in plant-based food preparation. We use them like we would use dairy, on breakfast cereal, in drinks, as bases for sauces, in smoothies, cakes, and many more recipes.

Try to get into the habit of soaking nuts every night, so you will always have fresh milk. For example, soak cashews for 2 to 6 hours. Remember to rinse well after soaking and discard the water you soaked the nuts in and use fresh water to blend.

Blend with fresh filtered water in a high speed blender on high at a ratio of 3 parts water to 1 part nuts or seeds.

Pour the blended liquid through a nut milk bag or fine mesh strainer lined with cheesecloth into a large bowl and squeeze and press to extract as much nut milk as possible.

Store the nut milk in a sealed container in the refrigerator for up to 4 days. If you can't make homemade milk, look for the store version with the least amount of preservatives, is GMO and carrageenan free, and unsweetened.

—

BREAKFAST

—

CHOCOLATE DREAM BOWL

Who doesn't love chocolate?! We wanted to create a healthy version of a naughty breakfast by adding superfoods and fermented foods into your daily dose.

EQUIPMENT
—

High speed blender
Measuring spoons
Measuring cups
Cookie dough scoop
Knife
Spatula

INGREDIENTS
—

CHOCOLATE BOWL

60-125ml (¼-½ cup) coconut water
1 tablespoon raw cacao powder
3 tablespoons coconut yogurt
1 teaspoon maple syrup
Pinch of Himalayan salt
4 medium frozen bananas (2 cups diced banana)

TOPPING

3-4 slices fresh banana
2 cookie dough scoops of roasted peanut butter (see recipe, page 37)
2 tablespoons VIBE granola (see recipe, page 34)
Goji berries

METHOD
—

Put all the ingredients in a blender using as much coconut water as you need to get your preferred consistency.

Pour into bowls and decorate with the toppings. Enjoy immediately.

Serves 1 - 2

// INGREDIENT SPOTLIGHT

Cacao VS Cocoa – What's the difference?

While cacao and cocoa start from the same place, the way they are processed has different effects on their nutritional benefits. "Cacao" refers to any of the products derived from the cacao bean that have remained raw. These products include cacao nibs, cacao butter, cacao mass or cacao paste, but most commonly cacao powder.

Raw cacao powder is made by cold-pressing unroasted cacao beans, this process retains the living enzymes and removes the fat (cacao butter). "Cocoa" looks the same but has been roasted at high temperatures, lowering the overall nutritional value, sometimes processed with Alkali that gives the powder a noticeably darker color, less acidic and more mellow flavor.

SLOW ROASTED VIBE GRANOLA

Our granola is the talk of the town, with many customers asking us for our secret recipe, so here it is. We choose to roast our granola slowly, although it takes longer, you will get a perfectly crispy granola, plus healthy fats are maintained when cooking at low temperatures.

EQUIPMENT
—

High speed blender
Measuring cups
Measuring spoons
Spatula
Large baking sheet
Baking parchment

INGREDIENTS
—

2 tablespoons dried raisins, soaked and drained
2 tablespoons dried currants, soaked and drained
2 tablespoons goji berries, soaked and drained
1 cup old fashioned rolled oats
½ cup raw almonds, chopped
½ cup raw pecans, chopped
½ cup raw cashews, chopped
¼ cup raw pumpkin seeds
¼ cup raw sunflower seeds
¼ cup coconut flakes
⅛ teaspoon sea salt flakes
½ cup dates, pitted and soaked in warm water for 15 minutes, drained
1 tablespoon apple cider vinegar
1 tablespoon maple syrup
¼ teaspoon ground cinnamon
2 tablespoons cold pressed coconut oil, melted

METHOD
—

Preheat the oven to 120°C (250°F). Line a baking sheet with baking parchment.

Combine rolled oats, nuts, seeds, coconut flakes and sea salt flakes in a large bowl. Add soaked raisins, currants and goji berries.

Blend soaked dates in ¾ cup filtered water (175ml) with apple cider vinegar, maple syrup, ground cinnamon and melted coconut oil in a blender until smooth and creamy. Transfer to the bowl with the oat mixture and stir to combine until fully coated.

Evenly spread the granola on the baking sheet and bake, stirring every 10 minutes, for 45-60 minutes or until golden brown. Remove and transfer to a flat tray to cool.

After cooling, break up any clumps and transfer to a tightly sealed container and store in the refrigerator for up to 1 month.

Note: Reconstitute the dried raisins, currants and goji berries by soaking them in hot water until they look plump, approximately 20 minutes or so and then drain them.

Serves 10 - 12

// TIPS FROM OUR CHEFS

Baking granola is like cooking cookies, in the sense that it continues baking when you pull it from the oven. If you don't want a really browned granola, trust your eyes and intuition when judging if it is ready to come out of the oven, it is always a surprise how much it crisps as it cools.

// TIPS FROM OUR CHEFS

Make the butter while the nuts are warm, as even more natural oils and flavor will be released.

Food processors and blenders, even top of the line home models can burn out, and simply shut off. Incorporating little breaks give the machine and also the mixture a chance to cool down before you add the oil and salt.

SIMPLE TOAST

ROASTED NUT BUTTER // SPICED MANGO COMPOTE

Making your own ingredients from scratch is a great place to start if you have just begun your journey into plant-based eating. These simple recipes are not only the building blocks for a lot of desserts, smoothies and dressings, but also for your day-to-day. Never throw away your empty glass jars, you can always store your creations in them like these nuts butters and compote.

EQUIPMENT
—

High speed blender or food processor
Baking sheet
Measuring cups
Measuring spoons
Spatula
Zester or grater
Knife
Fork

INGREDIENTS
—

ROASTED NUT BUTTER

2 cups raw and unsalted nuts
2 tablespoons cold pressed coconut oil, melted
¼ teaspoon Himalayan salt

SPICED MANGO COMPOTE

1 fresh ripe medium mango, chopped (about 1 cup)
1 tablespoon finely grated orange peel
1 tablespoon maple syrup
¼ teaspoon ground ginger
¼ teaspoon ground star anise
¼ teaspoon ground cinnamon
¼ teaspoon vanilla extract
⅛ teaspoon Himalayan salt

TO SERVE

1 slice of thick toast

METHOD
—

ROASTED NUT BUTTER

Preheat the oven to 160°C (325°F).

Place the nuts on a baking sheet and roast for 10-15 minutes, stirring once or twice, until fragrant and slightly golden brown.

If roasting hazelnuts or peanuts, transfer to a clean dish towel and rub the nuts to remove the skins.

Place the nuts in a blender or food processor and process at high speed for 2 minutes. Reduce to medium speed and process until the mixture has a creamy texture, and is smooth and velvety.

The mixture will go through different states, turning from whole nut, to meal, to powder, to clumps and then into creamy butter. This can take up to 10-12 minutes, so be patient and scrape the bowl frequently, especially at the start.

Once creamy, add coconut oil and salt and process for 1 or 2 additional minutes until it becomes completely smooth. Then transfer to a clean container and store in the refrigerator for up to 3 weeks.

SPICED MANGO COMPOTE

In a bowl mash the mango with a fork until it reaches your desire consistency.

Compotes can be served thick and chunky or pureed until smooth.

Add all the other ingredients and stir until well combined. Store in an airtight container in the refrigerator for up to 5 days.

ASSEMBLY

Lightly toast the bread and enjoy with your nut butter and spiced mango compote.

Serves 10 - 12

AMAZONIAN ACAI BOWL

We wanted to create a smoothie bowl that was more than just plain fruit, that's why our Acai Bowl is unusual and contains avocado. It is not only packed with essential mono-unsaturated healthy fats, avocado helps absorb the other antioxidants in the recipe and gives a creamy texture.

EQUIPMENT

High speed blender
Measuring cups
Measuring spoons
Knife
Spatula

INGREDIENTS

ACAI BOWL

60-125ml (¼ - ½ cup) coconut water
1 frozen packet of acai or
1 teaspoon acai powder + additional ½ cup frozen blueberries
½ ripe avocado
½ cup frozen blueberries
2 medium frozen bananas (1 cup diced banana)

TOPPINGS

2 purple dragon fruit hearts
2 tablespoons VIBE granola (see recipe, page 34)
Coconut shards
Goji berries
Chia seeds

METHOD

Put all the ingredients in a blender using as much coconut water as you need to get your preferred consistency.

ACAI BOWL

Pour into bowls and decorate with the toppings. Enjoy immediately.

Serves 1 - 2

// TIPS FROM OUR CHEFS

Making a smoothie or smoothie bowl is more than just accumulating ingredients into your blender. The way the ingredients are layered has an impact on the final texture. Adding liquids first, allows the blender to create a 'vortex', easily pulling down the rest of the components. Remember, the amount of liquid used will determine the consistency of your smoothie. Add only what your machine requires to get blending, otherwise you'll end up with a soup (albeit a delicious soup).

Frozen vs fresh banana - using frozen bananas you will give you a dense and creamy consistency and also, your bowl will be notably colder, staying firmer longer as you eat it. If you haven't had a chance to freeze your bananas beforehand, don't add coconut water. Fresh banana is typically enough to get your blender going and keep the acai at a thicker consistency.

COSMIC PARFAIT

OAT AND CHIA BIRCHER // BERRY COMPOTE // MANGO PUREE // VANILLA CASHEW CREAM

This is the perfect example of a nutritious breakfast, that's also delicious. The ingredients in this parfait can help lower blood sugar, sustain energy levels and are full of healthy fats, meaning it's a great way to start the day.

EQUIPMENT
—

High speed blender
Small saucepan
Measuring cups
Measuring spoons
Wooden spoon
Spatula
Knife

INGREDIENTS
—

OAT AND CHIA BIRCHER

1 cup old fashioned rolled oats
2 tablespoons chia seeds
1 ¼ cup nut milk
2 tablespoons fresh lemon juice
1 teaspoon maple syrup
⅛ teaspoon vanilla extract

BERRY COMPOTE

1 cup fresh or frozen mixed berries
2 teaspoons fresh orange juice
2 tablespoons maple syrup
1 tablespoon fresh lime juice

MANGO PUREE

½ fresh ripe medium mango, chopped (about 1/2 cup)
1 tablespoon fresh lemon juice
1 tablespoon maple syrup
⅛ teaspoon Himalayan salt

VANILLA CREAM

1 cup raw cashews, soaked
½ cup nut milk
¼ cup maple syrup
½ teaspoon vanilla extract
½ teaspoon mesquite powder (optional)
¼ teaspoon ground cinnamon
⅛ teaspoon Himalayan salt
2 tablespoons cold pressed coconut oil, melted

TO SERVE

Seasonal fruit salad
Slow roasted VIBE granola (see recipe, page 34)

METHOD
—

OAT AND CHIA BIRCHER

The night before, put oats and chia seeds into a container, pour over the milk, and add the maple syrup, vanilla and lemon juice. Mix well, then cover and pop into the refrigerator overnight.

BERRY COMPOTE

Place all ingredients in a small saucepan and bring to a simmer. Once bubbling, reduce to medium low heat and muddle the fruit with a wooden spoon. Continue cooking for about 8 to 10 minutes or until the berries have totally broken down and the liquid is glossy.

Remove from the heat and leave the compote to cool.

Store in a container in the refrigerator for up to 3-4 days.

MANGO PUREE

Blend all ingredients into a smooth puree. Add water if you need. Store in a container in the refrigerator for up to 3 days.

VANILLA CREAM

Blend cashews, nut milk, maple syrup, vanilla, mesquite, cinnamon and salt until it's smooth. With the blender running slowly, add coconut oil until well combined.

Store in a container in the refrigerator for up to 5 days.

ASSEMBLY

Layer berry compote into the bottom of 2 or 3 serving glasses. Spoon a layer of oat and chia bircher on top of this. Coat with mango puree and vanilla cream, and one more layer of oat and chia bircher. Top with vanilla cream.

Garnish with fresh seasonal fruit salad and our VIBE granola as a crumble if you want. Beautiful!

Serves 2 – 4

WONDER TOAST

GREEN PEA HUMMUS // RED RADISH // TOASTED SEEDS

This recipe is a great alternative to traditional avocado toast. Sometimes you can't find the perfect ripe avocado but you can always have peas in the freezer. Plus peas contain 5.6 grams more protein per cup compared to avocado. It can also be served as a hummus with crudités.

EQUIPMENT
—

Food processor or high speed blender
Small saucepan
Fine mesh strainer
Bowl
Kitchen towel
Measuring cups
Measuring spoons
Citrus juicer or squeezer
Spatula

INGREDIENTS
—

2 cups shelled fresh or frozen peas
2 tablespoons chopped fresh coriander
2 tablespoons chopped fresh chives
2 tablespoons chopped fresh mint
2 cloves garlic, finely chopped
2 tablespoons tahini
2 tablespoons extra virgin olive oil
1 freshly grated lime peel
Juice of 1 lime (about 2 tablespoons)
¼ teaspoon Himalayan salt
¼ teaspoon ground black pepper
¼ teaspoon ground cumin
¼ teaspoon hot red pepper flakes

TO SERVE

Thick sliced bread
Himalayan salt
Fresh tomato
2-3 tablespoons green pea hummus
Red radish
Coriander
Sliced red onion
Toasted pumpkin and sunflower seeds
Lime

METHOD
—

Boil salted water in a saucepan. While the water heats, prepare an ice bath by filling a deep bowl about halfway with water and ice.

When the water is boiling, add the peas and cook until tender, about 2-3 minutes for fresh peas or 3-4 for frozen.

Using a fine mesh strainer, drain the peas and immediately plunge them into the ice bath until cold (about 2 minutes). This halts the cooking process so the peas don't get mushy; it also preserves the vibrant color.

Drain the peas and place them on a clean kitchen towel to dry.

In a food processor or blender, pulse peas with the fresh herbs and garlic until fine and crumbled, pushing down the sides with a spatula as needed.

Add tahini, olive oil, lime peel, lime juice, salt, black pepper, cumin and red pepper flakes and blend until smooth but not puree. Place the green pea hummus in a serving bowl and season with more salt, black pepper, and lime juice, if desired. Store in an airtight container in the refrigerator for up to 4 days if not serving immediately.

ASSEMBLY

Toast the bread until lightly charred. Spread pea hummus on the toast. Top with red radish, tomato, sliced red onion, and seeds.

Serves 6 – 8

EGGLESS GREEN OMELETTE

HERB FILLING // ALMOND FETA // CASHEW SOUR CREAM

There is something about recreating egg dishes in vegan versions that is fun to do and comforting to eat. While these dishes don't taste exactly like eggs, they don't have to ~ they're delicious in their own right.

EQUIPMENT

—

High speed blender
Non stick frying pan (10 inches)
Bowl
Measuring cups
Measuring spoons
Long slotted spatula

INGREDIENTS

—

FLAX "EGG"

1 tablespoon ground flaxseeds
3 tablespoons warm filtered water

GREEN PASTE

¼ cup nut milk
2 tablespoons pesto (optional)
1 tablespoon extra virgin olive oil
1 tablespoon nutritional yeast
1 teaspoon chickpea miso
¾ teaspoon Himalayan black salt
¼ teaspoon ground turmeric
¼ teaspoon onion powder
¼ teaspoon garlic powder
⅛ teaspoon ground black pepper
½ cup spinach leaves, tightly packed
½ cup kale leaves, tightly packed
½ cup flat leaf parsley, tightly packed

CHICKPEA BATTER

1 cup chickpea flour
½ teaspoon baking powder
1 cup filtered water or vegetable stock (see recipe, page 49)

FILLING

Mix of green salad leaves
Shredded almond feta cheese (see recipe, page 66)
Slow roasted balsamic tomatoes, quartered (see recipe, page 66)

TO SERVE

Cashew sour cream (see recipe, page 57)
½ sliced avocado
Himalayan black salt
Ground black pepper
Living sprouts

METHOD

—

Soak 1 tablespoon of ground flaxseeds in 3 tablespoons of warm water and let sit for 10-15 minutes until it thickens.

In a blender, blend the green paste ingredients until smooth (approx. 2 minutes). We use cashew milk in this recipe, as it's rich and buttery, and most closely resembles the texture of dairy milk.

Whisk together the chickpea flour and baking powder. Slowly whisk in vegetable stock or water. The consistency should be something between a pancake and crepe batter. Add the green paste and whisk until smooth. Add the flax "egg" and combine. Let the batter rest for at least 10-15 minutes.

To cook, heat 1 tablespoon of olive oil in a non stick pan and spread evenly around the pan.

Add ¾-1 cup of green omelette batter to the pan, making sure to cover the pan fully and evenly.

Note: if your pan is smaller than 10 inches, use less batter.

Cook on medium to high heat. Wait until it bubbles and firms up at the edges (approx. 2 minutes or until just set underneath).

Add the filling to one side of the omelette. Use the spatula to gently fold over one side, creating an envelope and cook for 1 minute. Remove from the stove, cover with a lid and allow it to sit and steam for about 2-3 minutes.

ASSEMBLY

Serve with a spoonful of cashew sour cream, slices of avocado, black salt, freshly ground black pepper and living sprouts.

Serves 2

// TIPS FROM OUR CHEFS

Try to avoid buying pre-ground flaxseeds as they contain oils that are extremely perishable. When their ground, the oil begins to oxidize. This oxidation turns the oils rancid and impacts the aroma and flavor of your food. You can grind them using a coffee grinder or blender and store them in an airtight container in your refrigerator.

NEW YORK BAGEL

—

CHICKPEA SCRAMBLE // CHEESY CASHEW MAYONNAISE

—

The components of this recipe can be used in many different dishes, for example the vegetable stock can be used as the base of sauces and soups, and the cheesy mayonnaise is perfect slightly warmed over a plate of nachos. You can even omit the bagel and have a vegan scrambled chickpea "eggs".

EQUIPMENT
—

Large stockpot
Measuring cups
Measuring spoons
Fine mesh sieve or colander
High speed blender
Spatula
Bowl
Fork
Medium skillet or frying pan
Wooden spoon

INGREDIENTS
—

VEGETABLE STOCK

1 medium white onion, chopped (½ - ¾ cup)
1 medium carrot, chopped (½ - ¾ cup)
1 large celery stalk, chopped
1 tablespoon extra virgin olive oil
6 cups filtered water
1 dry bay leaf
1 clove garlic, smashed
1 whole clove
¼ teaspoon black peppercorns
3 thyme sprigs
5 parsley stems with leaves

"CHEESY" CASHEW MAYO

½ cup filtered water
2 tablespoons fresh lime juice
1 ½ tablespoon apple cider vinegar
1 ½ clove garlic, crushed
3 tablespoons nutritional yeast
1 tablespoon chickpea miso
1 teaspoon ground turmeric
1 teaspoon smoked paprika
½ teaspoon ground yellow mustard
½ teaspoon onion powder
¼ tsp Himalayan black salt
¼ tsp ground black pepper
2 cups raw cashews, soaked 8 hours
2 tablespoons extra virgin olive oil

CHICKPEA SCRAMBLE

2 medium yellow onion, finely chopped (about 1 ½-2 cups)
2 tablespoons extra virgin olive oil
1 teaspoon sea salt
1 large red bell pepper, finely chopped (about 1 cup)
1 ½ teaspoon ground turmeric
1 tablespoon smoked paprika
1 teaspoon ground cumin
1 teaspoon Himalayan black salt
½ teaspoon za'atar
¼ teaspoon ground black pepper
1 dry bay leaf
2 teaspoons apple cider vinegar
1 ½ cup vegetable stock
720g cooked chickpeas (about 4 ½ cups)

TO SERVE

Bagel
Lettuce
Tomato, sliced
Sliced avocado
Wilted spinach
Himalayan black salt
Freshly ground black pepper

METHOD
—

VEGETABLE STOCK

Roughly chop carrots, celery and onion into small diced pieces.

In a large stockpot, add olive oil and the vegetable mixture, stirring occasionally for 3 to 5 minutes.

Pour 6 cups of water into the pot. Add bay leaf, garlic, clove, and peppercorns. Bring to a boil over high heat, then simmer over low heat for 45 minutes.

Remove from the heat and add thyme and parsley. Cover and let it infuse for 20 minutes.

Set a fine mesh sieve or colander over another large pot or bowl and strain the stock. Discard the pulp. If you're not using it immediately, let it cool to room temperature, pour into a lidded container, cover, and refrigerate. Tightly sealed, the stock will keep for 5 days in the refrigerator and up to 6 months in the freezer.

"CHEESY" CASHEW MAYO

Blend all the ingredients apart from the cashews and olive oil in a blender until well combined. Add the cashews and blend until it's a smooth and thick creamy texture. Slowly drizzle in olive oil to finish. Store in a airtight container in the refrigerator for up to 1 week.

CHICKPEA SCRAMBLE

Place chickpeas in a mixing bowl and mash them with a fork until small and crumbly. You're looking for a chunky texture, not puree.

Over medium heat, saute onions with salt and olive oil for 5-7 minutes until soft. The salt helps to draw out moisture in the onions.

Add red pepper and continue cooking for 3-5 minutes. Add ground turmeric powder and cook for another minute, stirring constantly.

Add paprika, cumin, black salt, za'atar, black pepper and bay leaf, stirring to combine.

Add apple cider vinegar, and with a wooden spoon, get all the brown bits stuck to the bottom of the pan and cook until almost dissolved.

Add the stock, stir and cook on a low heat until the flavors combine (about 10-15 minutes).

Then add the chickpea scramble and cook, stirring frequently, until mostly dry and golden brown color. Be careful not burn the scramble.

Remove from the heat. If you intend to store the chickpea scramble for later, let it cool before refrigerating it, covered, for up to 3 days.

ASSEMBLY

Lightly toast a bagel and spread both sides with a spoonful of "cheesy" mayo. Serve with lettuce, slices of tomato, avocado, wilted spinach, and warm chickpea scramble.

Serves 6 - 8

—

MAIN COURSES

—

// TIPS FROM OUR CHEFS

Burger patties will keep in the refrigerator for up to 5 days, or you can freeze cooked burgers for up to a month. To reheat from frozen, preheat your oven to 190°C (375°F) and bake for 20–30 minutes or until heated through.

HONEST BURGER

BLACK BEAN BURGER // ROASTED TOMATO SAUCE

Our mission was to create a great tasting burger that is only made from whole foods; as often vegan burgers are made from processed 'mock meat' or tofu. As with all of our dishes, the nutritional content is important to us ~ protein from the black beans, vitamin E and magnesium from the almonds and fiber and vitamin A from red pepper, make this dish a nutritional powerhouse.

EQUIPMENT

—

High speed blender
Food processor
Measuring cups
Measuring spoons
Spatula
Bowl
Baking sheet

INGREDIENTS

—

ROASTED TOMATO SAUCE

500g ripe plum tomato
2 tablespoons extra virgin olive oil
1 teaspoon apple cider vinegar
¼ teaspoon Himalayan salt
1 large date, soaked for 10 minutes
¼ teaspoon paprika
1 clove garlic

BLACK BEAN PATTY

½ cup raw almonds
½ cup raw sunflower seeds
1 tablespoon extra virgin olive oil
4 cloves garlic, finely chopped
2 teaspoons ground cumin
1 teaspoon Himalayan salt
½ cup chopped coriander leaves, tightly packed
4 shallots, finely chopped (about ¼ cup)
1 long red bell pepper, finely chopped (about ½ cup)
240g cooked black bean (about 1 ½ cup)
2 tablespoons filtered water

TO SERVE

Burger bun
Lettuce
Tomato, sliced
Avocado, sliced

METHOD

—

ROASTED TOMATO SAUCE

Preheat the oven to 180°C (350°F).

Put the tomatoes on a baking sheet, drizzle with olive oil and roast for 45-60 minutes or until tender.

Peel tomato skins and discard them. Place the rest of the ingredients, including juices from the tomatoes in the blender and blend until smooth.

Let it cool completely then transfer to an airtight container in the refrigerator. They will last for up to 1 week.

BLACK BEAN PATTY

Combine almonds, sunflower seed, olive oil, garlic, cumin and salt in a food processor and pulse until breadcrumb texture. Add chopped coriander and pulse again until well combined.

In a mixing bowl, combine the onions and red pepper, then add the almond and sunflower mixture.

Transfer black beans to a food processor and add water. Pulse several times until it's smooth, then add it to the mixture.

Knead the mixture for a few minutes until it combines completely and place in the freezer for 30 minutes to set.

Preheat the oven to 180°C (350°F).

Form the mixture into 6 patties and place on an oiled baking sheet. Bake for 20-30 minutes or until just golden brown (flip after 10 minutes to bake evenly).

ASSEMBLY

Cut the buns in half and toast them if you like. Spoon a tablespoon of roasted tomato sauce on the base of each bun and add a layer of lettuce leaves, slices of tomato and avocado. Enjoy! You can play around with the toppings of your choice.

Serves 6

EXPLORER QUESADILLA

—

GUACAMOLE // ROASTED PUMPKIN // TOMATO SALSA // BEETROOT PICKLE //
CASHEW SOUR CREAM

—

*Our vegan, gluten free and super healthy version of one of the most delicious Mexican dishes. We put a VIBE spin on it
with probiotic pickles, and vegan sour cream. It is one of our best selling classics on the menu.*

EQUIPMENT

High speed blender
Medium non stick pan
1 liter wide mouth glass jar
Measuring cups
Measuring spoons
Citrus juicer
Zester or grater
Spatula
Bowl
Baking sheet
Knife

INGREDIENTS

FERMENTED PICKLED BEETROOT

6 cups shredded raw beetroot
1 ½ tablespoon sea salt
½ cup ginger, finely sliced
¼ cup parsley leaves, tightly packed
¼ orange peel

ROASTED PUMPKIN

1 small pumpkin, peeled, halved lengthwise, pitted, diced
2 tablespoons extra virgin olive oil
2 teaspoons sea salt

TOMATO SALSA

1 cup seeded, finely diced tomatoes
¼ cup finely diced red onion
⅓ cup chopped fresh coriander
2 cloves garlic, finely chopped
1 jalapeño, seeded and finely chopped
2 tablespoons fresh lime juice
¼ teaspoon Himalayan salt
⅛ teaspoon ground black pepper

CASHEW SOUR CREAM

¼ cup + 1 tablespoon filtered water
¼ cup + 1 tablespoon fresh lime juice
1 ½ tablespoon apple cider vinegar
1 ½ clove garlic, crushed
½ tablespoon yellow mustard seeds
¼ teaspoon Himalayan salt
¼ teaspoon ground black pepper
2 cups raw cashews, soaked 8 hours
2 tablespoons extra virgin olive oil

GUACAMOLE

2 medium ripe avocados
1 shallot, finely chopped
2 tablespoons freshly squeezed lime juice
1 tablespoon finely chopped coriander leaves
1 teaspoon Himalayan salt

TO SERVE

Corn tortilla
Smoked paprika
Fresh coriander leaves

METHOD

FERMENTED PICKLED BEETROOT

Combine beetroot and salt in a mixing bowl. Squeeze the salted beetroot with your hands to release all the juices. Let it sit for 5 minutes until water is released. Add the rest of the ingredients and combine.

Pack in a clean glass jar, pushing the beetroot down with force, ensuring juice covers it entirely. If there isn't enough juice, make a brine of 2 cups filtered water and ½ tablespoon of sea salt. Leave 1 inch (2.5cm) of space at the top for gases and expansion.

To keep the beetroot submerged in the brine, take a small glass or ceramic insert, to press down into the jar.

Cover tightly with a lid and ferment at room temperature for 3 to 7 days or until it has enough sourness for your taste. Burp jar daily. The rate of fermentation will be faster in a warm environment. Move to the refrigerator to slow the fermentation.

ROASTED PUMPKIN

Preheat the oven to 200°C (400°F). Drizzle the pumpkin with olive oil and sprinkle with salt. Bake for 20-25 minutes.

TOMATO SALSA

In a bowl, combine all the ingredients. Let it sit for 30 minutes, giving the flavors a chance to marinate, then taste again. Add more salt, lime juice or coriander if desired.

CASHEW SOUR CREAM

Blend all the ingredients except for cashews and olive oil in a high speed blender until well combined. Add the cashews and blend until smooth and thick creamy texture. Slowly drizzle in olive oil to finish. Store in airtight container in the refrigerator for up to 1 week.

GUACAMOLE

Halve the avocados. Remove the stone. Scoop out the avocado and mash in a bowl.

Combine the avocados with the rest of the ingredients.

ASSEMBLY

Heat 1 corn tortilla in a pan over medium heat. Top with all the ingredients as you like. Garnish with smoked paprika and fresh coriander leaves.

Serves 6 - 8

// TIPS FROM OUR CHEFS

Once you're all set with your homemade kimchi, it's time to experiment with new combinations. Why not try adding it to nachos and our "cheesy" mayo topped with coriander leaves or kimchi pancakes.

PEANUT BUTTER
KIMCHI SANDWICH

An unlikely combination we hear you say? Trust us, it's delicious. Kimchi is a Korean fermented condiment traditionally made with fish sauce, but we have made a vegan version. Its tangy, spicy, and savory taste pairs perfectly with the nuttiness and creaminess of peanut butter.

EQUIPMENT

High speed blender
1 liter wide mouth jar
Measuring cups
Measuring spoons
Spatula
Large bowl
Mandoline (optional)
Knife and chopping board
Gloves

INGREDIENTS

KIMCHI

1 small napa cabbage (Chinese cabbage) or ½ large head
½ large Korean radish or daikon, cut into thin strips
1 medium carrot, cut into thin strips
¼ red bell pepper, cut into thin strips
¼ cup red cabbage, shaved on mandoline or thinly sliced
½ tablespoon sea salt

SEASONING PASTE

¼ cup red bell pepper, chopped
2-3 cloves garlic, finely chopped
2 tablespoons fresh ginger, finely chopped
2 tablespoons maple syrup
1 tablespoon fresh green onion or scallions, finely chopped
½ tablespoon sea salt
1 ½ teaspoon gochugaru (Korean chili powder) or Hot red pepper flakes

TO SERVE

2 pieces thick sliced bread
Peanut butter (see recipe, page 37)
Lettuce
Tomato, sliced

METHOD

Separate and wash cabbage leaves thoroughly. Coarsely chop and place in a large bowl.

Sprinkle ½ tablespoon of salt onto the cabbage and massage firmly to pull water out to form a brine.

To create the paste you can use a food processor, blender or mortar and pestle. Process to a smooth paste, adding a splash of water if needed.

Add the other vegetables to the brined cabbage along with the paste. Mix together well to make sure all the vegetables are coated with the paste.

Pack the kimchi tightly into a sterilized jar, squeezing out most of the air bubbles as you pack the mixture in. Leave a 1 inch (2.5cm) space at the top of the jar, as the kimchi will expand as it ferments. Seal the jar and keep in a dry, cool and dark place.

Leave it for a minimum of 48 hours (up to 5 days) to allow it to ferment. You may see bubbles inside the jar and brine may seep out of the lid; place a bowl or plate under the jar to help to catch any overflow.

Check the kimchi once a day, pressing down on the vegetables with a spoon to keep them submerged under the brine. When the kimchi tastes ripe enough for your liking, transfer the jar to the refrigerator. It will taste best after 1 week.

Always use clean utensils when dipping into your kimchi.

Note: This is a basic kimchi to illustrate the process. Feel free to experiment with different vegetables and proportions and the spiciness level.

ASSEMBLY

To prepare the sandwich, spread each piece of bread with 2 to 3 tablespoons of peanut butter, add lettuce, slices of tomato and a generous dollop of kimchi.

Serves 10 - 12

MACRO BOWL

—

MISO TEMPEH // KIMCHI // PICKLED RADISH // PICKLED GINGER //
SEAWEED // SESAME + GINGER DRESSING

—

The way we build all of our bowls is a VIBE signature, we like to add a variety of textures and colors and always make sure to add fermented and sprouted ingredients. This nourishing bowl focuses on sea and land vegetables, ferments and is inspired by the landscape of Japan.

EQUIPMENT
—

High speed blender
Small frying pan
2 x 500ml glass jar
Measuring cups
Measuring spoons
Spatula
Large bowl
Mandoline (optional)
Knife and chopping board
Peeler

INGREDIENTS
—

RED PICKLED RADISH

10-15 medium size red radish, ends trimmed, thinly sliced
1 cup apple cider vinegar
½ cup rice vinegar
1 cup coconut sugar
2 teaspoons sea salt
2 teaspoons pink peppercorns
1 teaspoon yellow mustard seeds

PICKLED GINGER

150-200g fresh young ginger
½ teaspoon sea salt
½ cup apple cider vinegar
¼ cup rice vinegar
2 tablespoons coconut sugar
½ teaspoon sea salt
2 squares of dried kombu (optional)

SESAME AND GINGER DRESSING

⅓ cup neutral flavored oil, such as grapeseed
⅓ cup rice vinegar
2 tablespoons sesame oil
1 tablespoon tamari
1 tablespoon maple syrup
1 tablespoon toasted sesame seeds
2 teaspoons freshly grated ginger
1 clove garlic, finely chopped

SALAD

100g mixed greens
¼ carrot, cut into thin strips
¼ white radish, cut into thin strips
¼ red bell pepper, cut into thin strips

TO SERVE

3 pieces marinated tempeh plus coconut oil to fry
Cucumber
Kimchi (see recipe, page 59)
Cooked brown rice
Wild seaweed (we love dulse + kelp)
Toasted sesame seeds

METHOD
—

RED PICKLED RADISH

In a small saucepan over medium heat, combine vinegars, sugar and salt. Stir just until the sugar dissolves, 2 to 3 minutes. Remove from heat and let cool until lukewarm.

Carefully put the radish in a glass jar. Add pink peppercorn and mustard seeds. Pour the brine over the radish until they are submerged completely. Wait until the brine settles, then pour in as much additional brine as you can.

Cover with a lid and let it sit on the countertop for 8 hours. Move to the refrigerator and let sit for 1 more day. Kept chilled, the radish will keep for at least 3 weeks.

PICKLED GINGER

Using an inverted spoon, scrape off brown spots from the ginger. Use a sharp knife or a mandoline to slice the ginger into paper thin slices.

Sprinkle ½ teaspoon salt and set aside for 30 minutes to reduce its hardness.

About 10 minutes before the ginger finishes mellowing out, bring a kettle of water to a boil. When the ginger is done, pour the just boiled water over the ginger. Use enough water to cover the ginger. Gently stir and let sit for 1 minute to further reduce the harshness. Place into a mesh strainer. Don't rinse. Shake a few times to expel water, then transfer into a glass jar.

In a small pot, add the vinegars, salt, sugar and dried kombu and bring to a boil stirring once or twice to dissolve the sugar.

Remove from the heat and when it is slightly cool, pour the liquid into the jar with the sliced ginger. Close the lid, let it cool, then refrigerate. Depending on the ginger, it may be ready to eat in 1 to 3 days and keeps for up to 1 month.

SESAME AND GINGER DRESSING

Place all ingredients, except the oil in a blender. Blend on high until fully incorporated.

Reduce speed to low and slowly stream in the oil. Store in the refrigerator until ready to serve.

ASSEMBLY

In a small bowl, add 2 tablespoons of sesame and ginger dressing, 1 teaspoon of miso paste and 3 slices of tempeh and let it marinate for about 10 minutes. Heat coconut oil in a small frying pan and fry the tempeh for about 2-3 minutes per side, or until browned and crispy.

Place the salad in a bowl.

Cut the cucumber into thin strips using a vegetable peeler and roll it up. Arrange the pickled radish, pickled ginger, kimchi, cooked brown rice and fried tempeh around it. Top with soaked wild seaweed and toasted sesame seeds. Serve with sesame and ginger dressing.

Serves 6 - 8

EARTH TO TABLE BOWL

—

ALMOND FETA // QUINOA // GUACAMOLE // BEETROOT PICKLE // BROWN RICE //
ROASTED RED PEPPER // RASPBERRY VINAIGRETTE

—

This dish really embodies our 'eat the rainbow' philosophy ~ by combining grains, legumes, fermented food, raw vegetables, nuts and seeds, it contains the best the earth has to offer with plant-based sources of protein, fiber, and essential minerals.

EQUIPMENT
—

High speed blender
Mini springform pan or silicone molds
Medium saucepan
Baking sheet
500ml glass jar
Large bowl
Knife and chopping board
Measuring cups
Measuring spoons
Cling film
Spatula
Peeler

INGREDIENTS
—

ALMOND FETA CHEESE

Don't be put off by this cheese taking three days to make, the steps are simple.

Day 1
2 cups blanched almonds (soaked 8-12 hours)
1 cup kimchi brine, drained and clean
½ teaspoon sea salt

Day 2
1 ¼ cup filtered water
2 tablespoons agar powder

Day 3
6 cups filtered water
¾ cup sea salt

ROASTED RED PEPPER

4-5 red bell peppers
1 cup extra virgin olive oil
¼ cup apple cider vinegar
¼ teaspoon Himalayan salt
⅛ teaspoon ground black pepper

SLOW ROASTED BALSAMIC TOMATOES

500g ripe plum tomato (6-8 tomatoes)
1 tablespoon extra virgin olive oil
1 tablespoon balsamic vinegar
2 sprigs of fresh thyme
¼ teaspoon Himalayan salt
⅛ teaspoon ground black pepper

RASPBERRY VINAIGRETTE

½ cup fresh or frozen raspberries
¼ cup apple cider vinegar
¼ cup raw pumpkin seeds
2 tablespoons balsamic vinegar
2 tablespoons maple syrup
2 teaspoons ground yellow mustard seeds
1 teaspoon pink peppercorns
1 teaspoon onion powder
¼ teaspoon Himalayan salt
⅛ teaspoon ground black pepper
1 cup neutral flavored oil, such as grapeseed

SALAD

100g mixed green leaves
¼ carrot, cut into thin strips
¼ white radish, cut into thin strips
¼ red bell pepper, cut into thin strips

TO SERVE

Salad
Cooked chickpeas
Cooked brown rice
Cooked quinoa
Fermented pickled beetroot (see recipe, page 57)
½ roasted red pepper, cut into long strips
Guacamole (see recipe, page 57)
Activated almonds
Living sprouts

METHOD
—

ALMOND FETA CHEESE

Day 1

After soaking, drain and rinse the almonds well.

Blend in a blender with the kimchi brine and salt until smooth.

Pour in a container with a lid and leave on the counter to ferment for at least 24 hours or until it becomes tangy (but no longer than 48 hours). Check the progress every 12 hours.

Day 2

In a medium saucepan, whisk together water and agar powder. Bring to a simmer on low heat and continue whisking for 2 to 3 minutes, until the mixture appears to thicken. Remove from the heat.

When agar mixture has cooled slightly, but not to the point of setting, blend with the fermented cheese that you prepared on day 1.

Pour the cheese into a springform pan or silicone molds. Cover and refrigerate overnight to set.

Note: if you are using a springform pan, grease with coconut oil before you pour in the cheese.

Day 3

In a large bowl, whisk filtered water and salt until it is dissolved.

Turn the cheese out of the mold and place it in the brine. Let it sit at room temperature for 8 hours.

Transfer to an airtight container and pour the brine until the cheese is completely covered.

Keep in the refrigerator for up to 2 months.

ROASTED RED PEPPER

Preheat the oven at 240°C (475°F).

Put the peppers on a baking sheet and drizzle with 2 tablespoons of olive oil. Roast for 30-40 minutes, turning frequently, until the skins are blistered.

Transfer the red bell pepper to a bowl, cover with cling film and leave to cool. Peel off the skin and remove the stem, core and seeds and place in a glass jar.

In a mixing bowl mix the oil, vinegar, salt and pepper.

Pour the marinade onto the peppers and refrigerate for up 2 weeks.

SLOW ROASTED BALSAMIC TOMATOES

Preheat the oven to 150°C (300°F).

Combine olive oil and balsamic vinegar and mix well.

Put the tomatoes on a baking sheet and sprinkle salt, pepper and thyme.

Roast for 50-60 minutes or until the tomatoes are shriveled and soft.

Cool and keep in an airtight container in the refrigerator for up to 1 week.

RASPBERRY VINAIGRETTE

Blend all the ingredients except for the oil in a blender until well combined. Slowly drizzle in oil to finish. Store in an airtight container in the refrigerator for up to 1 week.

ASSEMBLY

Place the salad in a bowl. Arrange all the other elements as you wish and serve with the raspberry vinaigrette.

Serves 6 – 8

ASIAN NOODLES

ZUCCHINI NOODLES // PEANUT BUTTER + SRIRACHA DRESSING

Inspired by Asian street food, this dish is our interpretation of a cooked noodle dish you can find in most markets in Cambodia. It is a super quick dish to prepare and you can use the dressing for many different salads.

EQUIPMENT
—

High speed blender
Spiralizer, mandoline or julienne peeler
Large bowl
Knife and chopping board
Measuring cups
Measuring spoons
Spatula
Peeler

INGREDIENTS
—

ZUCCHINI NOODLES SALAD

1 zucchini, spiralized (ribbons or thin strips)
¼ carrot, cut into thin ribbons with a peeler
¼ red bell pepper, cut into thin strips
¼ orange bell pepper, cut into thin strips
½ cup red cabbage, cut into thin strips
1 green onion (white and green parts), thinly sliced
2 tablespoons chopped roasted peanuts
1 tablespoon chopped fresh coriander
1 tablespoon chopped fresh Thai basil
1 teaspoon freshly grated lime peel
½ small Thai chili, seeded and thinly sliced

PEANUT BUTTER AND SRIRACHA DRESSING

½ cup smooth roasted peanut butter (see recipe, page 37)
½ cup raw cashews
¼ cup tamari
4 tablespoons fresh lime juice
2 tablespoons maple syrup
1 tablespoons rice vinegar
1-2 tablespoons Sriracha sauce
1 tablespoon grated fresh ginger
½ tablespoon coconut sugar
2 teaspoons cold pressed sesame oil
⅛ teaspoon ground black pepper
1 clove garlic, finely chopped

TO SERVE

Coriander leaves
Toasted sesame seeds
Dried chili flakes
Lime wedge
Roasted peanuts

METHOD
—

PEANUT BUTTER AND SRIRACHA DRESSING

Combine all ingredients in a blender and run until smooth. Store in the refrigerator for up to 1 week.

Note: The sauce thickens on its own depending on the texture of your peanut butter. If you are making it ahead of time and it becomes a little bit too thick, mix in 2 or 3 tablespoons of filtered water.

ASSEMBLY

Place the zucchini noodles salad in bowl. Add 2 or 3 tablespoons of peanut butter and Sriracha dressing and combine. Place marinated salad on the bottom of the plate. Garnish with coriander leaves, toasted sesame seeds and dried chili flakes. Serve with lime wedge, a dollop of peanut butter and Sriracha sauce and chopped roasted peanuts.

Serves 2 – 4

// TIPS FROM OUR CHEFS

When you handle chili peppers it is really important to wear plastic or rubber gloves to protect your skin from the oils in the chilies, or handle them as little as possible and then immediately wash hands thoroughly in hot soapy water. With or without gloves, avoid direct contact with your eyes. And don't forget to wash the utensils and cutting board after use. The same advice applies for dried hot peppers, with one additional caution: when grinding them and heating, be careful not to inhale the fumes or let them waft into your eyes.

BBQ CAULIFLOWER BITES

CASHEW SOUR CREAM // BARBECUE SAUCE

Theses bites are a great dish to eat as a quick snack, or served with drinks to share with friends. We love to roast cauliflower because it deepens its mellow flavor, and gives it almost a nutty taste.

EQUIPMENT
—

High speed blender
Baking sheet
Parchment paper
Large bowl
Knife and chopping board
Measuring cups
Measuring spoons
Spatula

INGREDIENTS
—

CAULIFLOWER BITES

1 large head cauliflower (about 3 cups of florets)
1 cup rice flour
½ cup cashew milk
½ cup filtered water
2 teaspoons garlic powder
1 teaspoon ground cumin
1 teaspoon paprika
¼ teaspoon Himalayan salt
¼ teaspoon ground black pepper
⅛ teaspoon cayenne pepper

BBQ SAUCE

1 cup roasted tomato sauce (see recipe, page 53)
2 tablespoons apple cider vinegar
2 tablespoons coconut sugar
2 tablespoons maple syrup
1 tablespoon extra virgin olive oil
½ tablespoon tamari
½ tablespoon smoked paprika
1 teaspoon yellow mustard seeds
1 teaspoon liquid smoke (optional)
½ teaspoon ground cumin
¼ teaspoon dried oregano
¼ teaspoon dried thyme
¼ teaspoon red chili flakes
⅛ teaspoon ground cinnamon
⅛ teaspoon ground allspice
1 clove garlic, finely chopped

TO SERVE

Cashew sour cream (see recipe, page 57) for dipping

METHOD
—

CAULIFLOWER BITES

Preheat the oven to 220°C (425°F).

Line a baking sheet with parchment paper.

Cut the cauliflower into four quarters through the core. Cut into bite sized pieces. All the florets should be uniformly sized to ensure that they cook evenly. You can also roast the stalk and core, they are edible too.

In a blender, combine the rest of the ingredients to make a thick batter.

In a large bowl, dip the cauliflower florets in the batter, coating fully and lay on the prepared baking sheet.

Bake for 15-25 minutes, or until the batter is golden. For even browning, flip halfway through.

Remove from the oven and brush BBQ sauce over the florets. Pop them back in the oven for another 8-10 minutes.

The BBQ sauce will be sticky and will be just beginning to blacken in some areas.

Serve hot with cashew sour cream.

BBQ SAUCE

Place all the ingredients into a medium saucepan and whisk to combine. Simmer for 5 to 10 minutes or until thickened.

Transfer the sauce to a blender and blend until smooth.

Let it cool completely, then transfer to an airtight container in the refrigerator for up to 1 week.

Serves 4 – 6

// TIPS FROM OUR CHEFS

Buy heads of cauliflower with tight, firm florets, without any discoloration. The leaves should look green and fresh. Avoid any heads with brown spotted florets and yellowish leaves.

At VIBE, we also use raw cauliflower as an alternative grain in our tabbouleh.

You can prepare cauliflower "rice" by tossing the florets into a food processor and processing until broken down and rice-like. If you don't have a food processor, you can use a large box grater.

Use a nut milk bag or mesh strainer to strain out excess water.

NUM PANG TEMPEH

—

KAMPOT BLACK PEPPER MARINATED TEMPEH // TUCK TREY CHILLI MAYO //
GREEN PAPAYA + CARROT PICKLE

—

If you go to the riverside in Phnom Penh at sunset, you will see the area come alive with kites, balloons and games of shuttlecock, you will also see street sellers of everything from popcorn to fried insects and barbecued skewers of meat. It's this traditional street food that inspired us to create this dish. We marinate the tempeh and cook it to recreate the barbecue taste. We made it into a baguette as they are everywhere in Cambodia, a legacy left over after years of French rule. Cambodians usually eat these baguettes for breakfast with a cup of strong coffee with condensed milk.

EQUIPMENT
—

High speed blender
Medium saucepan
Small saucepan
Large bowl
Knife and chopping board
Measuring cups
Measuring spoons
Spatula
Peeler

INGREDIENTS
—

KAMPOT BLACK PEPPER AND GINGER MARINATED TEMPEH

1 cup tamari
½ cup maple syrup
¼ cup fresh lime juice
2 tablespoons vegan "fish" sauce
½ tablespoon chili paste
1 tablespoon sea salt
1 ½ tablespoon palm sugar
3 tablespoons freshly ground black pepper
2 cloves garlic, finely chopped
1 tablespoon fresh ginger, finely chopped
18 slices of tempeh

CAMBODIAN COLESLAW

¼ head napa cabbage, finely shredded
⅛ head red cabbage, finely shredded
15g bean sprouts
½ red bell pepper, thinly sliced
5 Thai basil leaves
10 coriander leaves
1 tablespoon roasted peanuts, crushed
2 tablespoons Tuk Trey sauce

TUK TREY SAUCE

1 ½ cup warm water
½ cup vegan "fish" sauce
¼ cup rice vinegar
½ cup palm sugar
2 tablespoons clove garlic, finely minced
1 ½ tablespoon sea salt
3 - 4 Thai chilies
1 whole fresh lime, juiced

VEGAN "FISH" SAUCE

2 cups filtered water
3 tablespoons tamari
7g dried shiitake mushrooms
1 piece (5 x 10cm) sheet of dried kombu or wakame seaweed
½ shallot, chopped
2 cloves garlic, crushed
1 teaspoon black peppercorn
1 teaspoon chickpea miso paste
1 teaspoon tomato ketchup
¼ teaspoon palm sugar
½ teaspoon Himalayan salt

SAMBAL OELEK CASHEW MAYO

¼ cup + 1 tablespoon filtered water
¼ cup + 1 tablespoon fresh lime juice
1 ½ tablespoon apple cider vinegar
¼ teaspoon + 1 pinch Himalayan salt
¼ teaspoon ground black pepper
1 tablespoon chili paste
2 cups raw cashews, soaked 4 hours
2 tablespoons extra virgin olive oil

GREEN PAPAYA AND CARROT PICKLE

1 ¼ cup apple cider vinegar
¾ cup rice or white vinegar
½ cup palm sugar
1 teaspoon Himalayan salt
1 bird's eye chili (optional)
1 clove garlic, finely chopped (optional)
½ green papaya, finely shredded
2 carrots, peeled and finely shredded

METHOD
—

BLACK PEPPER AND GINGER MARINATED TEMPEH

In a medium saucepan, combine tamari, maple syrup, lime juice, "fish" sauce, salt and palm sugar. Stir to combine, then bring to a boil over medium heat. Reduce to low heat and simmer until the mixture has reduced by half (about 10-12 minutes).

Stir in the pepper, ginger and garlic, cook for 1 minute, then turn off the heat. Once it cools, it will be about the consistency of maple syrup.

Slice the tempeh, and fry 3 or 4 slices per sandwich with a little bit of oil until browned, 2 to 4 minutes, both sides. Add 3 or 4 tablespoons of the black pepper marinade and cook for 2 to 3 minutes.

CAMBODIAN COLESLAW

Mix all together in a bowl and let it sit in the liquid for 10 minutes to marinade.

TUK TREY SAUCE

Combine all the ingredients in a bowl and stir until the sugar is dissolved. Keep in a container in the fridge.

VEGAN "FISH" SAUCE

Bring all to a simmer in a medium pot, uncovered, over medium heat. Simmer until reduced by half. You should have about 1 cup of liquid. Strain, discard the pulp and keep in the fridge.

SAMBAL OELEK CASHEW MAYO

In a blender, mix water, lime juice, apple cider vinegar, salt, black pepper and chili paste until combined.

Then add the cashews and blend until it has a smooth texture. With the blender running slowly, add the olive oil and blend until combined.

GREEN PAPAYA AND CARROT PICKLE

Combine vinegar, salt and sugar in a small saucepan and bring to a boil and stir until the sugar and salt is dissolved. Remove from the heat and set aside.

In a bowl, add the brine and the chili, garlic, papaya and carrots and set aside for 2 hours. Then place in a container in the refrigerator.

ASSEMBLY

To prepare the sandwich, spread each piece of bread with 2 to 3 tablespoon of mayo, add tempeh, lettuce, salad, cucumber strips, pickles and herbs. Yummy! ឆ្ងាញ់ - changnyang

Serves 4 – 6

// ABOUT THE CREATION OF THIS DISH

This dish was created by our kitchen team in Siem Reap with the guidance of Carolina, our Executive Chef.

DESSERTS

MINI HEALTHY DONUTS

These are great to make with children, letting them dip them in chocolate and top with different things. In our cafes, we top them with seeds but you can use natural colored sprinklings for birthdays. I always have a batch of these in the freezer for when I want a quick snack on the run.

EQUIPMENT
—

Food processor
Measuring cups
Measuring spoons
Spatula
Bowl
Silicone mini donut mold
Tray
Parchment paper

INGREDIENTS
—

DOUGH

1 cup raw almonds
2 ½ cups pitted dates
½ teaspoon Himalayan salt
1 tablespoon cold pressed coconut oil, melted

CHOCOLATE COATING

½ cup cold pressed coconut oil, melted
¼ cup + 2 tablespoons maple syrup
1 ½ tablespoon raw cacao powder
2 tablespoons cacao butter, melted

TOPPINGS

Shredded coconut
Pumpkin seeds
Goji berries
Chia seeds

METHOD
—

DOUGH

Place the almonds in the food processor and pulse until you achieve a powdery consistency.

Add the dates and salt, process again until the mixture sticks together and forms a doughy texture, stopping to scrape the sides down a few times. With the food processor running, add coconut oil.

Press the mixture into the silicone mini donut molds and freeze for at least one hour to firm up.

CHOCOLATE COATING

In a mixing bowl, stir together melted coconut oil and maple syrup until combined.

Add the raw cacao and whisk until you get a smooth consistency. Add melted cacao butter and repeat the same process. You will get a silky and thick coating.

ASSEMBLY

Dip the donuts in the chocolate coating, place on a tray lined with parchment paper and add your toppings.

Transfer to the refrigerator for at least 30 minutes until the chocolate is set. We challenge you to eat only one!

Serves 15 – 20

MACA CHILI TRUFFLES

Raw desserts are often the gateway to plant-based eating for a lot of people. They're easy to make and often taste so delicious, that it's hard to tell it from the real thing.

EQUIPMENT
—

High speed blender or food processor
Measuring cups
Measuring spoons
Spatula
Hotel pan or flat airtight container
Tray
Parchment paper

INGREDIENTS
—

3 cups raw cashews
½ cup maple syrup
½ teaspoon vanilla extract
¼ cup warm water
1 tablespoon maca powder
¼ teaspoon Himalayan salt
¼ teaspoon freshly ground nutmeg
⅛ teaspoon cayenne pepper
½ cup + 1 tablespoon cacao butter, melted
½ cup + 1 tablespoon raw cacao powder, plus extra to coat

TOPPING

Raw cacao powder

METHOD
—

In a blender process the cashews until you get a thick butter. Add the rest of the ingredients, apart from the cacao butter and cacao powder.

With the blender running slowly, pour in the melted cacao butter and cacao powder and blend until well combined. Do not over blend or overheat, once the cacao is added to the mixture, it will to separate.

Place the mixture in a flat container and refrigerate for 3-4 hours to firm.

Scoop the mixture into individual balls and roll them in cacao powder. You can use a cookie scoop for evenly sized balls.

Place on a plate or baking tray lined with baking paper and leave in the fridge for 2 hours.

Once set, store in a sealed container in the fridge for up to 1 week or 1 month in the freezer.

Serves 10 - 15

// TIPS FROM OUR CHEFS

You will notice as you make these cookies a few times, that they tend to fall into one of two categories, chewy or crumbly. This is because of the exact consistency of the peanut butter. With practice you will get the best of both worlds, cookies that are crisp on the edges and chewy in the center.

PEANUT BUTTER COOKIES

These cookies are one of the VIBE classics. We are completely addicted to them. Peanuts are a staple in Khmer cuisine, we slow roast them in house in nano batches to intensify the natural aroma and sweetness of peanuts and to ensure freshness.

EQUIPMENT

Food processor or high speed blender
Measuring cups
Measuring spoons
Spatula
Bowl
Cookie cutter (optional)
Baking tray
Parchment paper

INGREDIENTS

FLAX "EGG"

1 tablespoon ground flaxseeds
3 tablespoons warm filtered water

2 cups roasted peanuts, peeled
½ teaspoon baking soda
¾ cup coconut or palm sugar
½ teaspoon Himalayan salt

METHOD

Soak 1 tablespoon of ground flaxseeds in 3 tablespoons of warm water and let it sit to thicken for 10-15 minutes before adding to the recipe.

In a food processor or blender, add the roasted peanuts until it becomes a crunchy thick butter, stopping to scrape the sides down a few times.

Stir together the crunchy peanut butter, baking soda, palm sugar and salt in a medium bowl until the mix sticks together and forms a doughy texture. Add the flax "egg" and stir until well combined.

Place the dough in the refrigerator for 1 hour or until set.

Preheat the oven to 180°C (350°F). Line a baking tray with parchment paper.

Remove the dough from the fridge and press into the cookie cutter or working with 2 tablespoons of dough at a time, roll into balls and place on the prepared baking sheet. Press each dough ball.

Bake for 10 to 12 minutes, or until set on top, golden brown on the bottom and slightly brown around the edges, but not on top (cookies will not look fully baked), rotate baking tray halfway through baking.

Let cookies cool on a baking sheet for 5 minutes; transfer to wire rack and let cool to room temperature.

These cookies will last for 10 days in an airtight container in the refrigerator. They can be frozen for up to a month.

Serves 10 - 15

MEDICINAL ENERGY BALLS

These energy balls are a non-bake super easy way to start incorporating superfoods and adaptogens into your diet. They are also the perfect post workout recovery snack.

EQUIPMENT
—

Food processor
Measuring cups
Measuring spoons
Spatula
Bowl
Tray
Parchment paper

INGREDIENTS
—

½ cup buckwheat seeds
½ cup dry shredded coconut
½ tablespoon chia seeds
½ tablespoon flaxseed powder
½ teaspoon Schisandra powder (optional)
¼ teaspoon ground cinnamon
¼ teaspoon ground ginger
¼ teaspoon sumac (optional)
⅛ teaspoon vanilla powder
¼ teaspoon Himalayan salt
1 tablespoon brown tahini
2 tablespoons fresh orange juice
½ teaspoon maple syrup
½ cup pitted dates, chopped, soaked in warm water for 10 minutes
½ cup mixed dried berries (goji, mulberries and golden berries), soaked in warm water for 10 minutes

TOPPING

½ cup freeze dried raspberries, ground into powder (optional)
White sesame seeds

METHOD
—

Place the buckwheat seeds in the food processor and pulse until you achieve a meal consistency, making sure it's not too fine. Add the shredded coconut, seeds and the spices and process again until well combined.

Add tahini, orange juice and maple syrup and pulse again.

Add the dates and dried berries, process again until the mixture sticks together and forms a dough texture, stopping to scrape the sides down a few times.

Place the dough in the refrigerator for 30 minutes or until set.

Scoop out the dough into small balls, then roll them in raspberry powder. You can use a cookie scoop for evenly sized balls.

Place on a plate or baking tray lined with baking paper and leave in the fridge for 2 hours. Once set, store in a sealed container in the fridge for up to 1 week or 1 month in the freezer.

Serves 10 - 15

// INGREDIENT SPOTLIGHT

*Schisandra is a plant and the fruit is used
as an adaptogen for alleviating fatigue,
enhancing physical performance and endurance.
Additionally, Schisandra is used for improving
vision and muscular activity and preventing
motion sickness, offering great benefits
for athletes.*

// TIPS FROM OUR CHEFS

The remaining bar dough leftover can be reshaped into energy balls!

RAW YOGI BAR

This creation was born because a lot of our customers wanted a snack pre and post workout. We packed it with slow releasing carbohydrates which are an effective source of energy.

EQUIPMENT

High speed blender
Food processor
Measuring cups
Measuring spoons
Fine mesh sieve
Spatula
Square baking pan
Parchment paper

INGREDIENTS

½ cup old fashioned rolled oats
1 ½ cup toasted sunflower seeds
1 ½ cup toasted pumpkin seeds
½ teaspoon ground cinnamon
¼ teaspoon ground nutmeg
¼ teaspoon ground ginger
½ cup pitted dates, soaked in warm water for 15 minutes
2 ripe bananas (about 2 cups sliced)
2 tablespoons coconut butter
1 ½ tablespoon cold pressed coconut oil
¼ teaspoon vanilla extract
½ cup puffed quinoa
¾ cup currants

TOPPING (OPTIONAL)

Nut butter (see recipe, page 37)
Fresh sliced banana

METHOD

Line a 15cm (6 inches) square baking pan with parchment paper.

In a blender process the oats into a fine flour. Sieve the flour into a large mixing bowl using a fine mesh sieve.

Process seeds, spices and salt into a fine meal in the food processor and add to the oat flour.

Place the drained dates in the blender with the bananas, coconut butter, coconut oil and vanilla extract until you have a smooth paste.

Pour the date and banana paste into the dry mixture and thoroughly combine until it forms a dough. Add puffed quinoa and currants and mix again.

Press the mixture into the prepared pan and flatten it out. Tightly cover the pan with plastic wrap and refrigerate overnight.

Lift the mixture out of the pan and slice into bars. Individually wrap the bars in plastic sandwich wrap and refrigerate to store for up to 1 week.

ASSEMBLY

Spread nut butter and add slices of banana on top of a bar.

Serves 10-15

RASPBERRY CREAM CHEESECAKE

Our raw cheesecakes is one of our most popular dishes, it's unbelievable that it contains no dairy as the cashews are so creamy. It's a great dish to take to a dinner party and not tell anyone it's vegan to see their reactions.

EQUIPMENT

Food processor
High speed blender
Stand mixer or hand mixer
Springform cake tin
Parchment paper
Measuring cups
Measuring spoons
Fine mesh colander
Spatula
Bowl

INGREDIENTS

BASE

1 ¼ cup raw almonds
¼ cup shredded coconut
⅛ teaspoon Himalayan salt
1 cup pitted dates

FILLING

2 (400ml) cans full fat coconut milk, refrigerated overnight
2 cups raw cashews, soaked 8 hours
½ cup maple syrup
2 tablespoons freshly grated lime peel
¼ cup fresh lime juice
1 teaspoon vanilla extract
⅛ teaspoon Himalayan salt
¾ cup cold pressed coconut oil, melted

RASPBERRY SWIRL

1 cup fresh or frozen raspberries
2 tablespoons coconut or palm sugar

METHOD

Line a 20cm (8 inches) springform cake tin with parchment paper and chill your mixing bowl in the freezer before use.

BASE

In a food processor, pulse all the ingredients except for the dates into a fine crumble. Add the dates and process until a dough forms.

Spread the crust over a parchment lined cake tin and place it in the refrigerator for 30 minutes.

RASPBERRY SWIRL

Puree in a blender the raspberries with sugar. Strain the mixture through a fine mesh colander, in order to separate the seeds from the pulp. Discard the seeds.

FILLING

Take the chilled coconut cream and mixing bowl out of the refrigerator. Carefully scoop the thick layer of solid coconut cream from the top into a bowl, leaving the liquid behind. Use a stand mixer or a hand mixer to whip the cream until peaks form. It will take 3 or 4 minutes till the cream becomes light and fluffy.

In the blender, blend the rest of the ingredients apart from the coconut oil until smooth. Reduce the speed to low and slowly stream in the coconut oil. Pour the cheesecake mix over the coconut whipped cream and mix until combined.

Pour the filling on top of the almond crust. Drizzle the raspberry mixture to create a swirl pattern.

Freeze the cake for at least 4 hours. Then either keep it frozen and thaw out before serving, or transfer and keep refrigerated for up to 3 days.

Makes 1 cake

TIRAMISU

—

COFFEE LATTE MILK // COFFEE SYRUP // MOCHA LAYER // COCONUT BASE

—

Our take on an Italian classic ~ it tastes creamy, light and is refined sugar free and completely raw.

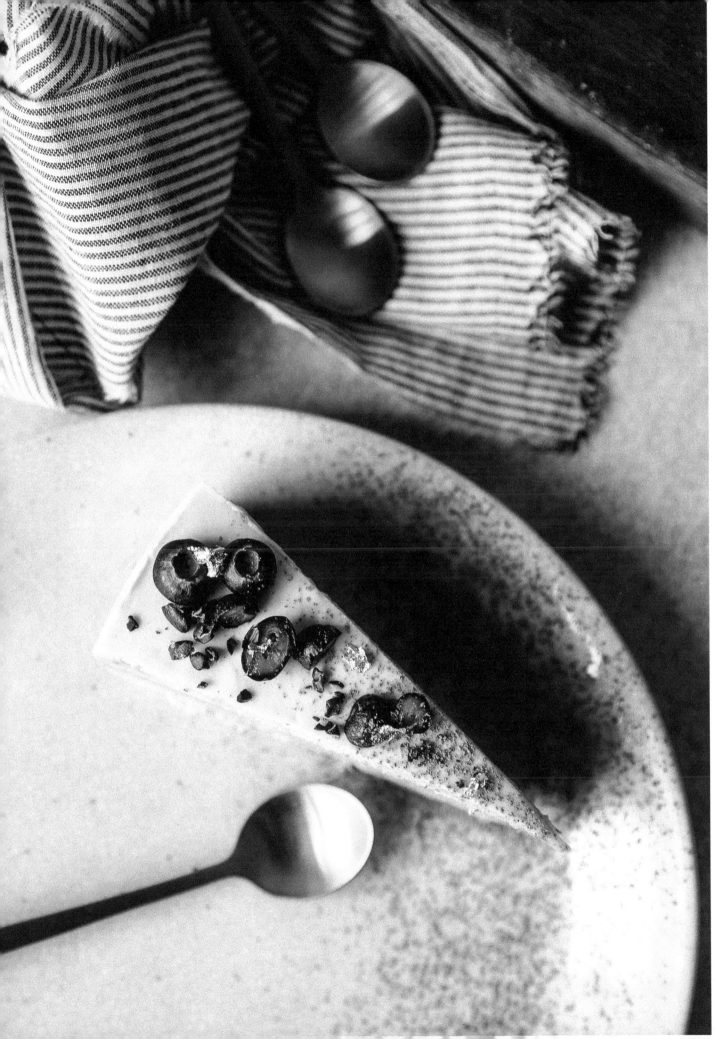

EQUIPMENT
—

High speed blender
Springform cake round pan
Nut milk bag
Parchment paper
Measuring cups
Measuring spoons
Spatula
Bowl

INGREDIENTS
—

COFFEE SYRUP

½ cup freshly brewed strong coffee
¼ cup maple syrup
2 tablespoons coconut syrup (see recipe, page 18)
2 tablespoons cold pressed coconut oil

COFFEE "LATTE" MILK

2 cups raw almond, soaked 6 hours
1 ½ cup filtered water
1 cup strong cold brew coffee
⅛ teaspoon Himalayan salt

BASE

1 cup coconut flour
1 teaspoon mesquite (optional)
⅛ teaspoon Himalayan salt
2 cups almond coffee "latte" pulp
½ cup coffee syrup

MOCHA LAYER

1 cup coffee "latte" milk
¾ cup cold brew coffee
½ cup maple syrup
½ cup raw cacao powder
¼ teaspoon vanilla powder
¼ teaspoon Himalayan salt
⅛ teaspoon ground coffee
3 cups raw cashews, soaked 8 hours
1 ½ cup coconut meat
1 ¼ cup cold pressed coconut oil

CHEESECAKE LAYER

½ cup agave
Peel of ½ lemon
¼ cup fresh lemon juice
1 tablespoon chickpea miso
½ tablespoon nutritional yeast
⅛ teaspoon Himalayan salt
2 cups raw cashews, soaked 8 hours
½ cup cold pressed coconut oil, melted
2 tablespoons cacao butter, melted

TOPPINGS

Raw cacao powder
Chocolate coating (see recipe, page 79)
Fresh blueberries (optional)

METHOD
—

Line a 20cm (8 inches) springform cake tin with parchment paper.

COFFEE SYRUP

Put all the ingredients in a blender on a very low speed until well combined.

Transfer to a clean jar and store in the refrigerator up to 2 weeks.

COFFEE "LATTE" MILK

Blend all the ingredients in a blender on high for 1 minute. Using a nut milk bag, strain the milk and reserve the pulp for the crust and the milk for the mocha layer.

BASE

In a mixing bowl combine coconut flour, mesquite and salt. Add the pulp and syrup and hand mix all the ingredients.

Press the crust over a parchment lined cake tin and place it in the refrigerator for 30 minutes or until well set.

MOCHA LAYER

Blend all the ingredients apart from the cashews, coconut meat and coconut oil in a blender until well combined.

Add the cashews and the coconut meat and blend until it's smooth, with a thick and creamy consistency. Slowly drizzle in coconut oil to finish. Pour the mocha mixture into the prepared base and quickly transfer to the freezer for at least 4 hours or until well set.

CHEESECAKE LAYER

Blend all the ingredients apart from the cashews, coconut oil and cacao butter in a blender until well combined. Add the cashews and blend until it's smooth and creamy consistency. Slowly drizzle in coconut oil and finish adding the melted cacao butter.

Pour the cheesecake mixture over the mocha layer. Place in the freezer for 4 hours or until well set.

Freeze the completed cake for at least 4 hours. Then either keep it frozen and thaw out before serving, or transfer and keep refrigerated for up to 5 days.

Serve with the toppings as you like.

Makes 1 cake

NAHM KRUK PANNA COTTA

—

DRAGON FRUIT + PUMPKIN PANNA COTTA // COCONUT + SESAME CRUMBLE

—

Nahm Kruk ~ Dessert in Khmer language. Cambodia's traditional desserts are mostly made from red bean, rice, banana, coconut and pumpkin. They usually wrap them in banana leaves and are sold in markets and on the roadside.

// ABOUT THE CREATION OF THIS DISH

This dessert was developed by our kitchen team in Phnom Penh with the help of Carolina, our Executive Chef.

EQUIPMENT

High speed blender
Medium saucepan
Food processor
Measuring cups
Measuring spoons
Spatula
Silicone molds
Large baking sheet
Parchment paper

INGREDIENTS

PANNA COTTA

Pumpkin layer
¼ cup maple syrup
1 teaspoon vanilla extract
¼ teaspoon Himalayan salt
100g fresh mango
100g roasted pumpkin (see recipe, page 57)
30g coconut meat
2 cups filtered water
½ cup palm sugar
2 teaspoons agar powder
2 teaspoons chia seeds

Dragon fruit layer
210g red dragon fruit
190g fresh mango
20g coconut meat
50g roasted pumpkin (see recipe, page 57)
2 teaspoons apple cider vinegar
1 teaspoon vanilla extract
⅛ teaspoon salt
1 cup filtered water
¼ cup + 1 tablespoon palm sugar
2 teaspoons agar powder

COCONUT AND SESAME CRUMBLE

Flax "egg"
2 tablespoons ground flax seeds
½ cup warm filtered water

1 cup roasted peanuts
1 cup coconut shards
1 cup sesame seeds
½ cup palm sugar
¼ cup maple syrup
1 teaspoon vanilla extract
2 teaspoons ground cinnamon

TO SERVE

Dragon fruit
Mango
Homemade coconut syrup (see recipe, page 18)
Khmer sweet basil leaves
Edible flowers
Basil seeds

METHOD

PANNA COTTA

For the pumpkin layer, blend in a blender maple syrup, vanilla extract, salt, mango, roasted pumpkin and coconut until smooth.

In a medium saucepan, whisk together water and agar powder. Bring to a simmer on low heat and continue whisking for 2 to 3 minutes, until the mixture appears to thicken. Remove from the heat.

When agar mixture has cooled slightly, but not to the point of setting, blend with the pumpkin mixture until well combined. Add chia seeds and blend again.

Divide the mixture into the prepared silicone molds (depending on size it will determine how much is in each mold). Cover and refrigerate overnight or until set (at least 2 hours).

When the first layer has set, blend the next layer in a blender consisting of dragon fruit, mango, coconut, roasted pumpkin, apple cider vinegar, vanilla extract and salt until smooth.

In a medium saucepan, repeat the same step from the pumpkin layer.

When agar mixture has cooled slightly, but not to the point of setting, blend with the dragon fruit mixture until well combined.

Remove silicone molds from the fridge and pour the mixture on top of the pumpkin layer. Cover and refrigerate overnight or until set (at least 4 hours). The finished panna cotta will keep, refrigerated, up to 5 days.

COCONUT AND SESAME CRUMBLE

Preheat the oven to 120°C (250°F). Line a baking sheet with baking parchment.

Soak ground flaxseeds in warm water and let sit for 10-15 minutes until they thickens.

Combine maple syrup, vanilla extract and cinnamon in a bowl. Add soaked ground flaxseeds and whisk until combined.

In a food processor pulse roasted peanuts, coconut shards and sesame seeds to break into smaller pieces. Transfer to the bowl with the wet mixture and stir to combine until fully coated.

Evenly spread the granola on the baking sheet and bake, stirring every 10 minutes, for 45-60 minutes or until golden brown. Remove and transfer to a flat tray to cool.

After cooling, break up any clumps and transfer to a tightly sealed container and store in the refrigerator for up to 1 month.

ASSEMBLY

Invert the mold over a dessert plate. We like to service it with fresh mango, dragon fruit, coconut syrup, crumble, basil leaves and flowers.

Serves 14 - 16

TONICS & ELIXIRS

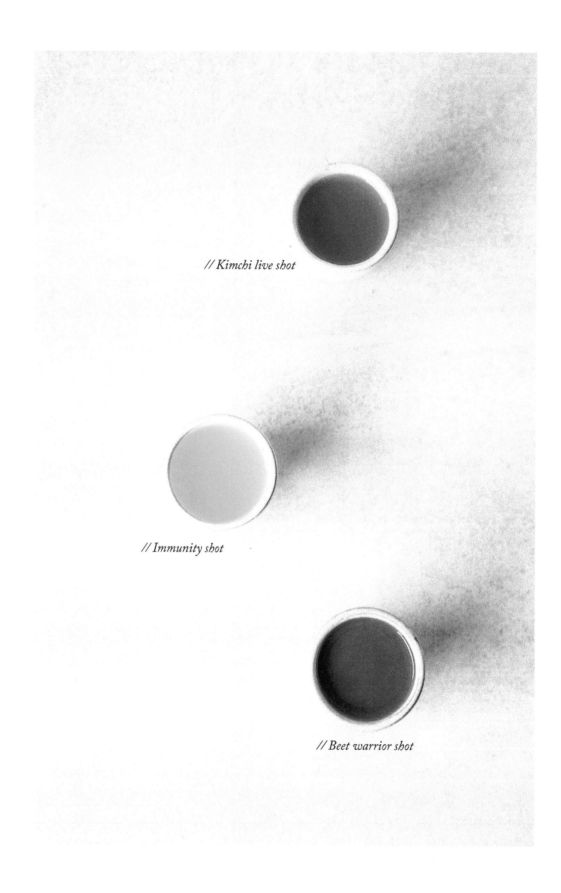

// Kimchi live shot

// Immunity shot

// Beet warrior shot

VIBE LIVE SHOTS

We often use these shots as the first line of defense if we are feeling under the weather or run down. These immunity boosting shots have fermented brines to boost the probiotics in the gut, oil of oregano for skin health and turmeric root for its well publicized anti-inflammatory properties.

EQUIPMENT

—

Juicer
Measuring cups
Measuring spoons
Citrus juicer or squeezer

INGREDIENTS

—

KIMCHI LIVE SHOT

2 tablespoons kimchi brine
1 tablespoon liquid gold juice (see recipe, page 113)
½ tablespoon fresh lime juice
¼ teaspoon fresh ginger juice or ⅛ teaspoon ground ginger
⅛ teaspoon cayenne pepper

BEET WARRIOR SHOT

2 tablespoons fermented beetroot brine
1 tablespoon warrior juice (see recipe, page 117)
½ tablespoon fresh orange juice
¼ teaspoon fresh turmeric juice or ⅛ teaspoon ground turmeric
⅛ teaspoon ground black pepper

IMMUNITY SHOT

2 tablespoons aloe vera juice
1 tablespoon fresh lemon juice
1 teaspoon fresh ginger juice
¼ teaspoon oil of oregano

METHOD

—

Add all the ingredients to a small jar and whisk until combined.

Pour into a shot glass and drink up!

Serves 1

// TIPS FROM OUR CHEFS

I like a little shot of this to start the day, but you can also dilute the fermented brine with water for a less sour drink, or mix a shot of it in dressings, sauces, smoothies or mocktails, like "kimchi bloody Mary" with tomato and bell pepper juice, celery, lime, black pepper and crushed ice.

// INGREDIENT SPOTLIGHT

Butterfly pea is an amazing brain boosting herb native to tropical equatorial Asia that it has been consumed for centuries as a memory enhancer, brain booster, anti-stress and calming agent. Known for its luminous indigo color, butterfly pea has traditionally been used as a vegetable in cooking and to color desserts.

ROYAL ELIXIR

Butterfly pea ~ a Cambodian classic ingredient infused with some next level blue magic with the addition of moringa, lemongrass, ginger and coconut water. It may become your new favorite happy hour drink!

EQUIPMENT

Measuring cups
Measuring spoons
Fine mesh sieve
Small saucepan

INGREDIENTS

MORINGA AND BUTTERFLY PEA INFUSION

4 cups filtered water
¾ cup fresh chopped lemongrass stalk
¾ cup fresh chopped ginger root
¼ cup palm or coconut sugar
2 tablespoons dried moringa leaves
1 tablespoon dried gotu kola leaves (optional)
¼ cup dried butterfly pea flower

SERVED

Crushed ice
Mint leaves
½ cup moringa and butterfly pea infusion
3 tablespoons fresh lime juice
Coconut water

METHOD

MORINGA AND BUTTERFLY PEA INFUSION

Bring the water, lemongrass, ginger and sugar to a boil in a small saucepan, stirring until the sugar has dissolved.

Reduce to a medium heat and simmer, uncovered for 25 minutes.

Add moringa leaves and butterfly pea flowers and bring to a boil. Once boiling, turn off the heat.

Steep for 10 minutes, then strain the infusion through a fine mesh sieve. Leave to cool at room temperature.

You can store it for up to 2 weeks, in a sterilized bottles in the refrigerator.

ASSEMBLY

Serve immediately over crushed ice, mint leaves, lime juice and top with coconut water.

Serves 5

SUMMER NIGHTS COOLER

When creating this elixir, we imagined a balmy summers night with the smell of sea and sand in the air. This cooler would make a great mocktail at a party.

EQUIPMENT

Juicer
Measuring cups
Measuring spoons
Fine mesh sieve
Small saucepan
Long glass

INGREDIENTS

ROSEMARY AND GINGER SYRUP

1 ½ cup filtered water
½ cup maple syrup
50g fresh ginger root
10g fresh rosemary sprigs

SERVED

¼ cup fresh apple juice
2 tablespoons rosemary and ginger syrup
Tonic or sparkling water
Crushed ice

METHOD

ROSEMARY AND GINGER SYRUP

In a small saucepan, bring the water, ginger and maple syrup to a boil, stirring until the maple syrup has dissolved. Add the rosemary and reduce to a medium heat. Simmer for 15 minutes, or until a syrup consistency is achieved.

Strain the syrup through a fine mesh sieve. Leave to cool at room temperature. You can store it for up to 2 weeks, in a glass jar in the refrigerator.

ASSEMBLY

Add all the components over ice and serve.

Serves 1

// INGREDIENT SPOTLIGHT

Cardamom known as "the queen of spices" are the small triangular seed pods of Elettaria cardamomum which is related to ginger. The green pods have a strong, unique taste, with an intensely aromatic fragrance. It's used for food and drinks and also as a medicine. It is good for improving digestion, soothing stomach pains and relieving gas.

DR.DETOX ELIXIR

We originally created this drink using cardamom essential oil but when we considered our 'from scratch' philosophy, we knew we needed to even make this infusion ourselves. We also added additional spices from the original recipe for their healing qualities.

EQUIPMENT

Measuring cups
Measuring spoons
Frying pan
Medium saucepan
Pestle and mortar
Fine mesh sieve

INGREDIENTS

DETOX INFUSION

4 cups filtered water
20 cardamom pods
6 cloves
1 star anise
1 teaspoon fennel seeds
½ teaspoon coriander seeds
½ teaspoon cumin seeds

2 tablespoons dried lemon balm
¼ cup dried chamomile flowers

SERVED

Crushed ice
½ cup detox infusion
¼ teaspoon spirulina
Coconut water

METHOD

DETOX INFUSION

Toast the seeds and spices in a dry frying pan, over medium heat, until they become aromatic. Then lightly crush them with a pestle and mortar.

Add the toasted seeds and spices to boiling water in a saucepan. Simmer for 25 minutes.

Add chamomile flowers and dried lemon balm and bring to a boil. Once it's boiling, turn it off.

Steep for 10 minutes and strain the infusion through a fine mesh sieve. Leave to cool to room temperature.

ASSEMBLY

Serve immediately over crushed ice, spirulina and top with coconut water.

Serves 5

BEAUTY TONIC

The color red in plant-based nutrition signifies a high amount of lycopene which is known to protect against certain types cancers and lower the risk of heart disease. Plus we choose the berries in this tonic specifically for their skin healing properties.

EQUIPMENT

Measuring cups
Measuring spoons
Medium saucepan
Fine mesh sieve

INGREDIENTS

BEAUTY INFUSION

4 cups filtered water
¼ cup palm or coconut sugar
2 teaspoons goji berries
2 teaspoons buckthorn berries
2 teaspoons schisandra berries
2 teaspoons dried cherries
¼ cup dried hibiscus flowers

SERVED

Crushed ice
½ cup beauty infusion
3 tablespoons lime juice
¼ teaspoon rose water
¼ teaspoon apple cider vinegar
Sparkling water

METHOD

BEAUTY INFUSION

Bring the water and sugar to a boil in a saucepan, stirring until the sugar has dissolved.

Reduce to a medium heat and add all the berries and simmer uncovered for 25 minutes.

Add hibiscus flowers and bring to a boil. Once boiling, turn off the heat.

Steep for 10 minutes, then strain the infusion through a fine mesh sieve. Leave to cool at room temperature. Store for up to 2 weeks in the refrigerator.

ASSEMBLY

To serve, pour into a glass filled two thirds of the way with crushed ice, beauty infusion, lime juice, rose water, apple cider vinegar and top off with sparkling water.

Serves 1

// INGREDIENT SPOTLIGHT

Buckthorn berries are a great source of vitamin C, carotene, vitamin E, malic, succinic acids, and other bioactive compounds. They are a wonderful source of rare fatty acid omega-7 which can keep your skin looking firm and vibrant. A superfood for the skin!

SUPER TONIC

Refreshing and soothing, this tonic is like giving yourself a hug. It is really easy to make and you can keep it in the fridge on stand-by for when you want it. It would also be great with pomegranate for an extra hit of antioxidants.

EQUIPMENT

High speed blender
Measuring cups
Measuring spoons
Nut bag or fine mesh sieve

INGREDIENTS

5 cups seedless and chopped watermelon
4 cups coconut water
2 tablespoons fresh lime juice
2 tablespoons rose water
¼ cup + 2 tablespoons chia seeds

SERVED

Crushed ice
⅛ teaspoon Himalayan salt

METHOD

Puree the watermelon in a blender (or use a juicer).

Using a nut bag or fine mesh sieve carefully strain the liquid and discard the pulp if you use a blender.

Stir the watermelon juice in coconut water, lime juice, rose water and chia seeds. Chill, covered, for at least one hour or until cold.

ASSEMBLY

Serve immediately over ice. Top it with a pinch of Himalayan salt.

Serves 5 – 6

JUICES, SMOOTHIES & COLD MILKS

LIQUID GOLD JUICE

This vibrant gold juice is packed with so much potent nutrient power, it is a delicious combination filled with anti-inflammatory, energy boosting, and digestion soothing properties with our hero spice, turmeric that adds citrusy and peppery notes.

EQUIPMENT
—

Juicer
Knife
Scale
Chopping board

INGREDIENTS
—

10g fresh turmeric root
3 oranges, peeled
1kg carrot, peeled
1 pineapple

METHOD
—

Wash and roughly chop all the ingredients and feed them through your juicer, beginning with the turmeric root to allow the juice of the oranges and pineapple to push through the more fibrous root.

Pour into a glass and drink.

Serves 3 – 4

// TIPS FROM OUR CHEFS

Depending on the type of juicer you have, you may need to chop your ingredients into small pieces before juicing.

LIFE FORCE JUICE

Juicing can be a good way to get your five-a-day. For every 500ml of juice, you can be consuming up to 1kg of fruit and vegetables. We prefer to use more vegetables than fruit and keep our combinations simple.

EQUIPMENT
—

Juicer
Knife
Scale
Chopping board

INGREDIENTS
—

850g cucumber (peeled)
500g pear (peeled)
70g spinach
25g kale (stem and all)
20g parsley
1 tablespoon lemon juice

METHOD
—

Wash and roughly chop all the ingredients and feed them through your juicer, beginning with the spinach and kale to allow the juice of the cucumber and pears to push through the more fibrous root.

Pour into a glass and enjoy.

Serves 3 - 4

// TIPS FROM OUR CHEFS

Roll up leafy greens so they are denser and less likely to roll around and get stuck. Rotate soft and hard produce, like pears, to push through soft bits that they can stuck in the feeding tube of the juicer. Plus, the lemon juice will slow down the oxidation process.

// TIPS FROM OUR CHEFS

You can juice ginger, apples, carrots and beetroots with the peel if they are organic. Apple peel is rich in phytochemicals like phenolic acids and flavonoids, also it is a good source of calcium, potassium, folate, iron, vitamins A and C; beetroot peel is not yummy to eat but it blends pretty well, and has a nice earthy taste.

Citrus peels can get a little tricky, it has powerful antioxidants but at the same time the oils from the peel are hard on the digestive system.

THE WARRIOR JUICE

This juice is slightly sweet and perfectly balanced with a little kick from the ginger. It contains vitamins A, K and beta carotene from the carrots, vitamin C and polyphenols from apples, antioxidants and folate from the beetroot, and anti-inflammatory benefits from the ginger and ellagic acid and punicic acid from the pomegranate, both highly beneficial for cell regeneration.

EQUIPMENT

Juicer
Knife
Scale
Chopping board

INGREDIENTS

10g fresh ginger root
200g beetroot
3 apples
½ pomegranate
1kg carrots
1 lime, peeled

METHOD

Wash and roughly chop all the ingredients and feed them through your juicer, beginning with the ginger root to allow the juice of the beets and apples to push through the more fibrous root.

Pour into a glass and drink up!

Serves 3 - 4

CASHEW CHAI MILK

In India, drinking traditional chai tea is a core part of day-to-day life. Ours is a tea-free version that includes a warm spice blend. Chai is an ancient spice blend, all of which have their own superpowers, used to help relaxation, improve digestion and strengthen immunity.

EQUIPMENT

High speed blender
Measuring cups
Measuring spoons

INGREDIENTS

1 ½ cup cashew milk
6 dates, pitted and soaked
1 teaspoon cold pressed coconut oil
¼ - ½ teaspoon chai spice mix
¼ teaspoon vanilla extract
¼ teaspoon Himalayan salt

CHAI SPICE MIX

3 tablespoons ground cinnamon
2 tablespoons ground ginger
1 tablespoon ground cardamom
½ tablespoon ground allspice
½ tablespoon ground clove
½ tablespoon ground nutmeg
½ tablespoon ground black pepper
1 teaspoon ground star anise

METHOD

CHAI SPICE MIX

Combine the ground spices in a jar, mix well and store until ready to use.

ASSEMBLY

Add all the ingredients to the blender and process on low, then high for at least 1 minute or until well incorporated.

You can store it for up to 2-3 days, in a glass jar in the refrigerator.

Shake well before serving and pour into a glass filled two-thirds with ice. We love to drink it really cold but you can also serve warm.

Serves 1

// TIPS FROM OUR CHEFS

Add 1 large turmeric root, peeled and roughly chopped to the blender and you will get a golden chai cashew milk, including all the benefits from the curcumin.

SUPERFOOD CHOCOLATE MILK

Chocolate milk always reminds me of being a child and getting a treat. Now as an adult, it is still a treat but a healthy one. This is a non-dairy, gluten free, lactose free, no preservative or artificial colors, cholesterol-free milk. It is super nutritious with a silky and creamy texture, packed with protein, fiber, potassium, antioxidants and is a source of several important vitamins and minerals.

EQUIPMENT

—

High speed blender
Scale
Measuring cups
Measuring spoons
Mixing bowl or vessel
Spatula
Nut milk bag

INGREDIENTS

—

1 cup raw cashews, soaked 8 hours
2 cups filtered water
25g dates, pitted and soaked in warm water for 10 minutes
2 tablespoons raw cacao powder
1 tablespoon palm or coconut sugar
1 ½ teaspoon maca powder
1 ½ teaspoon cordyceps powder
1 ½ teaspoon chia seeds
1 ½ teaspoon cacao nibs
1 ½ teaspoon maple syrup
1 teaspoon ground cinnamon
½ teaspoon vanilla extract
½ teaspoon ground ginger
⅛ teaspoon Himalayan salt
1 pinch cayenne pepper (optional)

METHOD

—

Add all the ingredients to the blender and blend on low, then progress to high for at least 1 minute. The texture will be smooth and creamy.

Using a nut milk bag and large bowl, carefully pour the nut milk mixture through the bag, squeezing out all of the liquid. Discard the pulp. Be sure that the bag is perfectly sealed.

Shake well before serving and pour into a glass.

Serves 2

CAMBODIAN JUNGLE SMOOTHIE

This Cambodian inspired smoothie is the perfect combination between the sweetness from the mango, the tartness from the passion fruit and the spiciness from the turmeric.

EQUIPMENT
—

High speed blender
Spatula
Measuring cups
Measuring spoons

INGREDIENTS
—

1 ½ cup coconut water
1 cup frozen mango
1 passion fruit
½ fresh thumb size turmeric root, peeled
1 pinch ground black pepper

METHOD
—

Add all the ingredients to the blender and blend on low, then progress to high for at least 1 minute or until well incorporated.

Drink straight away in a glass filled two-thirds of the way with ice.

Serves 1

// TIPS FROM OUR CHEFS

You can substitute the fresh turmeric for 1 teaspoon of "turmeric paste" (see recipe, page 139).

If you're looking for a creamy milky texture or you can't find coconut water, you can add coconut milk to have a mango lassi experience.

EMMA'S CHOCOLATE SUPERFOOD SMOOTHIE

This was one of the first smoothie recipes I created when I opened my first little cafe nearly ten years ago and it has stuck on the menu in all of the subsequent cafes I've opened since.

EQUIPMENT

—

High speed blender
Measuring cups
Measuring spoons
Spatula

INGREDIENTS

—

1 ½ cup cashew milk
1 large banana, frozen (or 2 small)
2-3 medjool dates, pitted (optional)
1 ½ teaspoon cacao powder
1 teaspoon goji berries
1 teaspoon cacao nibs (optional)
⅛ teaspoon Himalayan salt

METHOD

—

Blend together milk, banana, dates, salt and cacao powder in the blender on low, then progress to high for at least 1 minute or until well incorporated and super smooth.

Add the cacao nibs and goji berries and blend for another 10 seconds or so - you want them to remain slightly crunchy.

Serve immediately in a glass over ice.

Serves 1

PURE LOVE SMOOTHIE

This is one of our best selling smoothies, its nutty, extremely filling and great if you want to show yourself some extra love.

EQUIPMENT

High speed blender
Measuring cups
Measuring spoons
Spatula

INGREDIENTS

1 ½ cup cashew milk
1 large banana, frozen (or 2 small)
3-4 medjool dates, pitted and soaked
2 tablespoons almond butter
1 teaspoon salted caramel
¼ teaspoon ground cinnamon

METHOD

Add all the ingredients to the blender on low, then progress to high for at least 1 minute or until well incorporated.

Serve it immediately over a glass of ice.

Serves 1

// TIPS FROM OUR CHEFS

We love cashew milk because it is the thickest, creamiest and most milk-like. It is really lovely with this recipe, but you can also try almond milk, mixed with other seeds to add more nutritional benefits, for example almond and hemp seeds (50/50).

—

MEDICINAL HOT DRINKS

—

// INGREDIENT SPOTLIGHT

ENERGIZING INFUSION

*Known for its anti-inflammatory and
antioxidant properties.*

HEALING INFUSION

*Excellent pain reducer and acts as an antiviral
and anti-microbial protector.*

REVIVE INFUSION

*Helps reduce high blood pressure and strengthen
the immune system.*

ENERGIZING, HEALING & REVIVE INFUSIONS

I have a personal love affair with tea. Not the type you get in tea bags from the supermarket that often contain fanning and dust but wildcrafted, organic tea from old trees and superior herbs and flowers for their medicinal benefits. Drinking tea is a mindful practice that can offer you a moment of peace and tranquility during a hectic day. All of the tea blends at VIBE have been crafted in-house by me with you in mind.

EQUIPMENT
—

Weighing scales
Small saucepan or kettle
Pot
Tea bags (optional) or unbleached muslin

INGREDIENTS
—

ENERGIZING INFUSION

2g dried turmeric root
2g dried ginger root
2g dried lemongrass

HEALING INFUSION

3g dried calendula flower
10g dried pau d´arco
3.5g dried cat's claw
20g goji berries

REVIVE INFUSION

10 leaves olive leaf
1.5g dried hibiscus flower
3.5g cinnamon stick

METHOD
—

Infusions, by definition, are "tea preparation from the more delicate plant parts, like the leaves and flowers and employs a steeping process to extract the beneficial components of the herb".

Simply place the loose tea in teabags, muslin or directly in a teapot and cover them with boiling water. If you can, use spring water as it can substantially improve the taste of the tea. Always use cold water, not preheated or overheated to avoid losing oxygen content. The level of oxygen is reduced if the water is boiled more than once. The ideal temperature for these infusions is between 97°C (208°F) to 100°C (212°F).

Allow to steep for 4-5 minutes, except for the healing infusion which should be simmered in a pot on the stove for 20 minutes and then drained of the pulp. This particular tea can also be used as the base for smoothies.

Serves 1

MEDICINAL CHAI LATTE

We're huge fans of adaptogens, we support the belief that they give us vitality of life and promote optimum health and longevity. We try to sneak them into our diet on a daily basis and this recipe is a great way to do that.

EQUIPMENT
—

High speed blender
Measuring cups
Measuring spoons
Small saucepan
Strainer

INGREDIENTS
—

1 ½ cup nut milk
¼ - ½ cup "chai chaga concentrate tea"
1 tablespoon maple syrup or 1 date
1 tablespoon almond butter
¼ teaspoon vanilla extract

CHAI CHAGA CONCENTRATE TEA

3 cups filtered water
½ teaspoon chaga powder
2.5cm piece fresh ginger root
6 whole cloves
2 cinnamon sticks
¼ teaspoon fresh grated nutmeg
10 black peppercorns
3 star anise whole
5 cardamom pods
½ fresh orange peel
3 tablespoons palm or coconut sugar

¼ cup black tea (Assam or Darjeeling tea)

TO SERVE

Ground cinnamon

METHOD
—

CHAI CHAGA CONCENTRATE TEA

In a saucepan put all the ingredients together apart from the tea. Over high heat, bring to a boil, then turn down to medium low heat and simmer, uncovered for 25 minutes. Stir every 5 minutes.

After 25 minutes, add the tea and bring to a boil, then turn off. Steep for 3 minutes, then strain.

Let the tea cool and keep in a sealed container. It should last for several weeks refrigerated.

ASSEMBLY

Heat the nut milk in a small saucepan until warm, but do not boil.

Combine with the rest of the ingredients in a blender, and blend for a minute. Pour into a mug and enjoy.

Note: you can prepare this drink as a iced latte adding a scoop of ice cubes.

Serves 1

// INGREDIENT SPOTLIGHT

Chaga, known as "the king of medicinal mushrooms" and the "mushroom of immortality", has anti-inflammatory and skin supporting properties, stimulates the immune system, promotes digestive support and is high in antioxidants and nutrients.

ADAPTOGEN LATTE

We created this recipe to help with stress and improve sleep that is so elusive in our modern busy world. Many of us suffer from exhausted adrenals and overstimulated stress responders, so this latte will sooth away your worries and help you to feel grounded.

EQUIPMENT

High speed blender
Measuring cups
Measuring spoons
Nut milk bag
Bowl
Small saucepan

INGREDIENTS

1 cup nut milk
¼ - ½ cup goji berry nectar
1 tablespoon maple syrup or 1 date
1 tablespoon almond butter
½ teaspoon ground Ashwagandha root
¼ teaspoon vanilla extract
¼ teaspoon ground green cardamom
⅛ teaspoon ground cinnamon
1 pinch ground clove

GOJI BERRY NECTAR

1 cup goji berries, soaked overnight
½ cup raspberries (optional)
2 cups filtered water

METHOD

GOJI BERRY NECTAR

Blend water, soaked goji berries and raspberries in a blender for a minute.

Pour it through a nut milk bag into a large bowl and squeeze and press to extract as much nectar as possible. Store the nectar in a sealed container in the refrigerator for up to 4 days.

Note: You can use this nectar as an alternative ingredient to enhance your recipes, for example in smoothies, dressings, sauces and desserts.

ASSEMBLY

Once ready to drink, heat the nut milk in a saucepan until warm, but do not boil. Combine with the rest of the ingredients in a blender, blending for a minute. Pour into a mug and enjoy when still warm.

Serves 1

// INGREDIENT SPOTLIGHT

GOJI BERRIES
Goji berries are natures highest source of natural melatonin, providing 15 mcg/oz. It is important to note that melatonin, unlike its precursor serotonin, is able to pass the blood brain barrier when ingested.

ASHWAGANDHA
Also known as Indian ginseng, is a root used in Ayurvedic medicine. It has emerged as one of the world's most powerful adaptogens. Ashwagandha supports healthy sleep by rejuvenating the body and addressing stress related exhaustion.

// INGREDIENT SPOTLIGHT

CORDYCEPS

Genus of parasitic fungi that grows on the larvae of insects – it has been used for centuries in traditional medicine as an adaptogen; fighting stress and fatigue and naturally increasing energy levels.

CHICORY

Known for supporting the liver and kidneys. Its bitter properties stimulate the appetite, increasing digestive enzymes and acids to increase nutrient absorption.

DANDELION ROOT

Useful digestive tonic as it helps to increase the flow of bile, which is important in the digestive process for the removal of waste product.

BURDOCK

Bitter herb used for skin conditions, general liver problems, a blood purifier and lymph cleanser.

ALTERNATIVE COFFEE

As much as we love coffee, we were getting many requests from guests for a coffee like drink but without the caffeine, so we developed our original alternative coffee to not only taste like coffee, it is also brimming with healing herbs and spices.

EQUIPMENT

High speed blender
Measuring cups
Measuring spoons
Fine mesh sieve
Small saucepan

INGREDIENTS

ALTERNATIVE COFFEE DECOCTION

1 tablespoon cordyceps powder
3 cups filtered water
2 tablespoons ground roasted chicory root
2 tablespoons ground roasted dandelion root
2 tablespoons ground roasted burdock root
1 cinnamon stick (optional)

TO SERVE

¼ - ½ cup alternative coffee decoction
1 cup nut milk
1 tablespoon almond butter
1 tablespoon maple syrup or 1 date (optional)

METHOD

ALTERNATIVE COFFEE DECOCTION

Bring the water and cordyceps to a boil in a saucepan, stirring until cordyceps has dissolved. Reduce heat to low-medium and add chicory, dandelion, burdock and cinnamon and simmer for 20-30 minutes or until the liquid is reduced by half.

Strain through a fine mesh sieve. Leave to cool at room temperature. You can store it for up to 1 week, in a glass jar in the refrigerator.

Note: you can roast the roots in a big batch following the same proportion. Once they've cooled, grind them finely in a coffee grinder or with a mortar and pestle and store in an airtight container.

Once ready to drink, heat nut milk and alternative coffee decoction in a saucepan until warm, but do not boil.

Combine with the rest of the ingredients in a blender, for a minute. Pour into mug and enjoy when still warm.

Serves 1

GOLDEN LATTE

Turmeric lattes are on trend right now, but often you're not assimilating the true benefits of the wonder herb. By combining turmeric with black pepper and healthy fats like coconut oil or nut butter, it enhances its bioavailability in the body, which increases the profound positive medicinal benefits it has to offer.

EQUIPMENT

—

High speed blender
Measuring cups
Measuring spoons
Small saucepan

INGREDIENTS

—

TURMERIC PASTE

½ cup ground turmeric
1 tablespoon ground ginger
1 cup filtered water
1 teaspoon ground black pepper
2 tablespoons cold pressed coconut oil, melted

SERVED

1 ½ cup nut milk
1 tablespoon almond butter
1 tablespoon maple syrup or 1 date (optional)
1 ½ teaspoon turmeric paste
½ teaspoon vanilla extract
⅛ teaspoon ground cinnamon
1 pinch Himalayan salt

METHOD

—

TURMERIC PASTE

Place water, turmeric, ginger, and black pepper into a saucepan and cook over low heat, stirring until it has reached a paste-like consistency, approximately 3-5 minutes.

Let the mixture cool, then add melted coconut oil and stir until well combined. Refrigerate in a sealed container. It should last for several weeks refrigerated.

ASSEMBLY

Heat nut milk in a small saucepan until warm, but do not boil.

Combine with the rest of the ingredients in a high speed blender, and blend for a minute. Pour into mug. Enjoy when it's still warm.

Serves 1

LUXURY HOT CHOCOLATE

What better way to treat yourself than with a creamy hot chocolate. Like all VIBE recipes, we took this to the next level by using unprocessed natural sweeteners and superfoods. This recipe is really easy to make on a rainy day, curled up with a good book.

EQUIPMENT
—

High speed blender
Small saucepan
Measuring cups
Measuring spoons

INGREDIENTS
—

1 ½ cup nut milk
3 tablespoons raw cacao powder
2 tablespoons maple syrup or 2-3 pitted dates
1 teaspoon mesquite powder (optional)
½ teaspoon vanilla extract
1 pinch Himalayan salt

SPICY

⅛ teaspoon cayenne pepper
Dash of cinnamon

EXTRA CREAMINESS

1 tablespoon almond butter

SUPERFOOD HOT CHOCOLATE

1 teaspoon maca powder

EXTRA PROTEIN BOOST

1 tablespoon hemp seeds

FOR A GORGEOUS LATTE

1 tablespoon tocotrienols powder

TO SERVE

Chocolate sauce (see recipe, page 79)

METHOD
—

Heat the milk in a saucepan until warm, but do not boil.

Combine with the rest of the ingredients in a blender for a minute. Pour into a mug and drizzle chocolate sauce for a luxury drink.

Note: We like to use a blender for these latte recipes because it heats as it blends to create a creamy smooth texture.

Serves 1

THE GOOD VIBE FOUNDATION

It was fundamental for us when we created VIBE that we also set up The Good Vibe Foundation, with the clear goal to provide health, food and education to school children in Cambodia and to be a positive impact in the world.

BACKGROUND

A beautiful country, full of genuine smiles, Cambodia is still recovering from a recent genocide. The average salary in 2016 was $3.30 per day and it is ranked the 35th poorest country in the world. It also has high rates of essential vitamin and mineral deficiencies. The World Health Organization ranks micronutrients deficiencies among the top ten leading causes of death globally. Cambodia also has a staggering 40% of stunted children according the latest Cambodian Demographic and Health Survey (CDHS 2010).

PROJECT

Our main project is 'Nourish for Learning' which aims to feed 10,000 school children healthy plant-based food in Cambodia. We work in poor, rural communities and hope to build long-term relationships with schools in order to commit to nourishing children throughout their education. We try to establish roots with the parents and families of the children to educate them on nutrition and give them practical knowledge and advice to help them feed healthier food to their children. We believe this community reach will impact the eating habits of several generations to come. We also work directly with farmers who produce fruit and vegetables without chemicals or pesticides, which allows us to serve high quality fresh ingredients.

Everytime you eat at VIBE, your money goes to support the Good Vibe Foundation.

Find out more about our organization at goodvibefoundation.org

TEAM

VIBE is the collaborative effort of many people who work passionately everyday to make it what it is. Our team is multicultural, drawing on their expertise to produce innovative plant-based cuisine.

EMMA FOUNTAIN
———

I created VIBE for people to have access to high vibrational food that is nourishing, healing and bursting with energy. I believe that natural food from the earth is our medicinal dispensary and we can experience optimal wellness by eating a diet that is mostly filled with plants. Affectionately known as the mother of VIBE, she's a global traveler, chef and training herbalist.

JAY FOUNTAIN
———

Having worked for many years in the hospitality world in the UK, Jay is the backbone of VIBE, keeping it humming like a well oiled machine. Without him, nothing at VIBE would be possible. Jay's super high standards and relentless striving for perfection for training our service team, help us provide the best possible experience to our customers.

CAROLINA RODRÍGUEZ CHINEA
———

I have always been passionate about the arts and food. Having worked extensively in the arts for many years, it gave me a passion for design and aesthetics and this lead me to become an International plant-based chef, developing recipes and creating kitchen concepts.

My love of food and its impact on my body has led me to be vegan. My life revolves around three concepts: learn, move and eat. My passion: think, feel and discover.

TEAMS IN CAMBODIA
———

We currently have around 50 members of our team in Cambodia and every single one of them plays a vital role in the running of our company. Their positive attitudes and commitment to our success is inspiring and heartwarming on a daily basis. Thank you Hies, Davon, Raksamy, Lina, Soksan, Sopaul, Laty, Linda, Srey Ni, Saramony, Khouch, Sophy, and many more...

First published in Cambodia 2018

ISBN 978-1-7327540-0-3

Text: Emma Fountain and Carolina Rodríguez Chinea
Recipe development: Emma Fountain and Carolina Rodríguez Chinea
Designer: Saat Studio
Photography, creative direction and styling: Nataly Lee

www.vibecafeasia.com

Food doesn't just fuel our body, it impacts how we feel throughout the day. What we eat affects our digestive health, skin radiance, energy levels but also our emotional body, our mood and motivation. We wanted a cafe concept which embraced, wholeheartedly, the powerful connection between mind and body. Our plant-based recipes are specifically designed using the healthiest of ingredients to extract the maximum nutritional value. We wanted to avoid faux health foods like tofu and focus instead on whole foods from the earth that we know are nutrient-rich and know exactly where they come from.

We believe eating a plant-based diet is the optimal way to nourish and care for the body and mind.

———

EMMA FOUNTAIN

$29.99
ISBN 978-1-7327540-0-3
52999>
9 781732 754003

CPSIA information can be obtained
at www.ICGtesting.com
Printed in the USA
LVHW070316040522
717923LV00005B/14